MW01294092

Legal Notice

BOOKS FROM THE GET 800 COLLECTION

28 New SAT Math Lessons to Improve Your Score in One Month
    Beginner Course
    Intermediate Course
    Advanced Course
New SAT Math Problems arranged by Topic and Difficulty Level
New SAT Verbal Prep Book for Reading and Writing Mastery
320 SAT Math Subject Test Problems
    Level 1 Test
    Level 2 Test
The 32 Most Effective SAT Math Strategies
SAT Prep Official Study Guide Math Companion
Vocabulary Builder
320 ACT Math Problems arranged by Topic and Difficulty Level
320 GRE Math Problems arranged by Topic and Difficulty Level
320 SAT Math Problems arranged by Topic and Difficulty Level
320 AP Calculus AB Problems
320 AP Calculus BC Problems
SHSAT Verbal Prep Book to Improve Your Score in Two Months
555 Math IQ Questions for Middle School Students
555 Advanced Math Problems for Middle School Students
555 Geometry Problems for High School Students
Algebra Handbook for Gifted Middle School Students

CONNECT WITH DR. STEVE WARNER

www.facebook.com/SATPrepGet800

www.youtube.com/TheSATMathPrep

www.twitter.com/SATPrepGet800

www.linkedin.com/in/DrSteveWarner

www.pinterest.com/SATPrepGet800

plus.google.com/+SteveWarnerPhD

320 SAT Math Problems arranged

by Topic and Difficulty Level

For the Revised SAT
March 2016 and Beyond

Steve Warner, Ph.D.

Table of Contents

ACTIONS TO COMPLETE BEFORE YOU READ THIS BOOK

1. Purchase a TI-84 or equivalent calculator

It is recommended that you use a TI-84 or comparable calculator for the SAT. Answer explanations in this book will always assume you are using such a calculator.

2. Take a practice SAT from the Official Guide to get your preliminary SAT math score

Use this score to help you determine the problems you should be focusing on (see page 9 for details).

3. Claim your FREE bonus

Visit the following webpage and enter your email address to receive additional problems with solutions.

www.thesatmathprep.com/320SATprmT1.html

4. 'Like' my Facebook page

This page is updated regularly with SAT prep advice, tips, tricks, strategies, and practice problems. Visit the following webpage and click the 'like' button.

www.facebook.com/SATPrepGet800

INTRODUCTION
THE PROPER WAY TO PREPARE

*T*here are many ways that a student can prepare for the SAT. But not all preparation is created equal. I always teach my students the methods that will give them the maximum result with the minimum amount of effort.

The book you are now reading is self-contained. Each problem was carefully created to ensure that you are making the most effective use of your time while preparing for the SAT. By grouping the problems given here by level and topic I have ensured that you can focus on the types of problems that will be most effective to improving your score.

1. Using this book effectively

- Begin studying at least three months before the SAT.
- Practice SAT math problems twenty minutes each day.
- Choose a consistent study time and location.

You will retain much more of what you study if you study in short bursts rather than if you try to tackle everything at once. So try to choose about a twenty-minute block of time that you will dedicate to SAT math each day. Make it a habit. The results are well worth this small time commitment.

- Every time you get a question wrong, **mark it off, no matter what your mistake**.
- Begin each study session by first redoing problems from previous study sessions that you have marked off.
- If you get a problem wrong again, **keep it marked off**.

Note that this book often emphasizes solving each problem in more than one way. Please listen to this advice. The same question is not generally repeated on any SAT so the important thing is learning as many techniques as possible.

Being able to solve any specific problem is of minimal importance. The more ways you have to solve a single problem the more prepared you will be to tackle a problem you have never seen before, and the quicker you will be able to solve that problem. Also, if you have multiple methods for solving a single problem, then on the actual SAT when you "check over" your work you will be able to redo each problem in a different way. This will eliminate all "careless" errors on the actual exam. Note that in this book the quickest solution to any problem will always be marked with an asterisk (*).

2. The magical mixture for success

A combination of three components will maximize your SAT math score with the least amount of effort.

- Learning test taking strategies that work specifically for standardized tests
- Practicing SAT problems for a small amount of time each day for about three months before the SAT
- Taking about four practice tests before test day to make sure you are applying the strategies effectively under timed conditions

I will discuss each of these three components in a bit more detail.

Strategy: The more SAT specific strategies that you know the better off you will be. Throughout this book you will see many strategies being used. Some examples of basic strategies are "plugging in answer choices," "taking guesses," and "picking numbers." Some more advanced strategies include "trying a simple operation," and "completing the square." Pay careful attention to as many strategies as possible and try to internalize them. Even if you do not need to use a strategy for that specific problem, you will certainly find it useful for other problems in the future.

Practice: The problems given in this book, together with the problems in the practice tests from the College Board's Official Study Guide (2016 Edition), are more than enough to vastly improve your current SAT math score. All you need to do is work on these problems for about ten to twenty minutes each day over a period of three to four months and the final result will far exceed your expectations.

Let me further break this component into two subcomponents – **topic** and **level**.

Topic: You want to practice each of the four general math topics given on the SAT and improve in each independently. The four topics are **Heart of Algebra**, **Geometry and Trig**, **Passport to Advanced Math**, and **Problem Solving and Data Analysis**. The problem sets in this book are broken into these four topics.

Level: You will make the best use of your time by primarily practicing problems that are at and slightly above your current ability level. For example, if you are struggling with Level 2 Geometry and Trig problems, then it makes no sense at all to practice Level 5 Geometry and Trig problems. Keep working on Level 2 until you are comfortable, and then slowly move up to Level 3. Maybe you should never attempt those Level 5 problems. You can get an exceptional score without them (higher than a 700).

Tests: You want to take about four practice tests before test day to make sure that you are implementing strategies correctly and using your time wisely under pressure. For this task you should use "The Official SAT Study Guide (2016 Edition)." Take one test every few weeks to make sure that you are implementing all the strategies you have learned correctly under timed conditions.

3. Practice problems of the appropriate level

Roughly speaking about one third of the math problems on the SAT are easy, one third are medium, and one third are hard. If you answer two thirds of the math questions on the SAT correctly, then your score will be approximately a 600 (out of 800). That's right—you can get about a 600 on the math portion of the SAT without answering a single hard question.

Keep track of your current ability level so that you know the types of problems you should focus on. If you are currently scoring around a 400 on your practice tests, then you should be focusing primarily on Level 1, 2, and 3 problems. You can easily raise your score 100 points without having to practice a single hard problem.

If you are currently scoring about a 500, then your primary focus should be Level 2 and 3, but you should also do some Level 1 and 4 problems.

If you are scoring around a 600, you should be focusing on Level 2, 3, and 4 problems, but you should do some Level 1 and 5 problems as well.

Those of you at the 700 level really need to focus on those Level 4 and 5 problems.

If you really want to refine your studying, then you should keep track of your ability level in each of the four major categories of problems:

- **Heart of Algebra**
- **Geometry and Trig**
- **Passport to Advanced Math**
- **Problem Solving and Data Analysis**

For example, many students have trouble with very easy Geometry and Trig problems, even though they can do more difficult Heart of Algebra problems. This type of student may want to focus on Level 1, 2, and 3 Geometry and Trig questions, but Level 3 and 4 Heart of Algebra questions.

4. Practice in small amounts over a long period of time

Ideally you want to practice doing SAT math problems ten to twenty minutes each day beginning at least 3 months before the exam. You will retain much more of what you study if you study in short bursts than if you try to tackle everything at once.

The only exception is on a day you do a practice test. You should do at least four practice tests before you take the SAT. Ideally you should do your practice tests on a Saturday or Sunday morning. At first you can do just the math sections. The last one or two times you take a practice test you should do the whole test in one sitting. As tedious as this is, it will prepare you for the amount of endurance that it will take to get through this exam.

So try to choose about a twenty-minute block of time that you will dedicate to SAT math every night. Make it a habit. The results are well worth this small time commitment.

5. Redo the problems you get wrong over and over and over until you get them right

If you get a problem wrong, and never attempt the problem again, then it is extremely unlikely that you will get a similar problem correct if it appears on the SAT.

Most students will read an explanation of the solution, or have someone explain it to them, and then never look at the problem again. This is *not* how you optimize your SAT score. To be sure that you will get a similar problem correct on the SAT, you must get the problem correct before the SAT—and without actually remembering the problem.

This means that after getting a problem incorrect, you should go over and understand why you got it wrong, wait at least a few days, then attempt the same problem again. If you get it right, you can cross it off your list of problems to review. If you get it wrong, keep revisiting it every few days until you get it right. Your score *does not* improve by getting problems correct. **Your score improves when you learn from your mistakes.**

6. Check your answers properly

When you go back to check your earlier answers for careless errors *do not* simply look over your work to try to catch a mistake. This is usually a waste of time. Always redo the problem without looking at any of your previous work. Ideally, you want to use a different method than you used the first time.

For example, if you solved the problem by picking numbers the first time, try to solve it algebraically the second time, or at the very least pick different numbers. If you do not know, or are not comfortable with a different method, then use the same method, but do the problem from the beginning and do not look at your original solution. If your two answers do not match up, then you know that this a problem you need to spend a little more time on to figure out where your error is.

This may seem time consuming, but that's okay. It is better to spend more time checking over a few problems than to rush through a lot of problems and repeat the same mistakes.

7. Take a guess whenever you cannot solve a problem

There is no guessing penalty on the SAT. Whenever you do not know how to solve a problem take a guess. Ideally you should eliminate as many answer choices as possible before taking your guess, but if you have no idea whatsoever do not waste time overthinking. Simply put down an answer and move on. You should certainly mark it off and come back to it later if you have time.

11

8. Pace yourself

Do not waste your time on a question that is too hard or will take too long. After you've been working on a question for about 30 to 45 seconds you need to make a decision. If you understand the question and think that you can get the answer in another 30 seconds or so, continue to work on the problem. If you still do not know how to do the problem or you are using a technique that is going to take a long time, mark it off and come back to it later if you have time.

If you do not know the correct answer, eliminate as many answer choices as you can and take a guess. But you still want to leave open the possibility of coming back to it later. Remember that every problem is worth the same amount. Do not sacrifice problems that you may be able to do by getting hung up on a problem that is too hard for you.

9. Attempt the right number of questions

Many students make the mistake of thinking that they have to attempt every single SAT math question when they are taking the test. There is no such rule. In fact, most students will increase their SAT score by *reducing* the number of questions they attempt.

There are two math sections on the SAT – one where a calculator is allowed and one where a calculator is not allowed. The calculator section has 30 multiple choice (mc) questions and 8 free response (grid in) questions. The non-calculator section has 15 multiple choice (mc) questions and 5 free response (grid in) questions.

You should first make sure that you know what you got on your last SAT practice test, actual SAT, or actual PSAT (whichever you took last). What follows is a general goal you should go for when taking the exam.

Score	MC (Calculator Allowed)	Grid In (Calculator Allowed)	MC (Calculator Not Allowed)	Grid In (Calculator Not Allowed)
< 330	10/30	3/8	4/15	1/5
330 – 370	15/30	4/8	6/15	2/5
380 – 430	18/30	5/8	8/15	2/5
440 – 490	21/30	6/8	9/15	3/5
500 – 550	24/30	6/8	11/15	4/5
560 – 620	27/30	7/8	13/15	4/5
630 – 800	30/30	8/8	15/15	5/5

For example, a student with a current score of 450 should attempt 21 multiple choice questions and 6 grid ins from the section where a calculator is allowed, and 9 multiple choice questions and 3 grid in questions from the section where a calculator is not allowed.

This is *just* a general guideline. Of course it can be fine-tuned. As a simple example, if you are particularly strong at Heart of Algebra problems, but very weak at Geometry and Trig problems, then you may want to try every Heart of Algebra problem no matter where it appears, and you may want to reduce the number of Geometry and Trig problems you attempt.

Remember that there is no guessing penalty on the SAT, so you should *not* leave any questions blank. This *does not* mean you should attempt every question. It means that if you are running out of time make sure you fill in answers for all the questions you did not have time to attempt.

10. Use your calculator wisely.

- Use a TI-84 or comparable calculator if possible when practicing and during the SAT.
- Make sure that your calculator has fresh batteries on test day.
- You may have to switch between DEGREE and RADIAN modes during the test. If you are using a TI-84 (or equivalent) calculator press the MODE button and scroll down to the third line when necessary to switch between modes.

Below are the most important things you should practice on your graphing calculator.

- Practice entering complicated computations in a single step.
- Know when to insert parentheses:
  - Around numerators of fractions
  - Around denominators of fractions
  - Around exponents
  - Whenever you actually see parentheses in the expression

Examples:

We will substitute a 5 in for x in each of the following examples.

Expression	Calculator computation
$\dfrac{7x+3}{2x-11}$	$(7*5+3)/(2*5-11)$
$(3x-8)^{2x-9}$	$(3*5-8)^\wedge(2*5-9)$

- Clear the screen before using it in a new problem. The big screen allows you to check over your computations easily.
- Press the **ANS** button (**2ND (-)**) to use your last answer in the next computation.
- Press **2ND ENTER** to bring up your last computation for editing. This is especially useful when you are plugging in answer choices, or guessing and checking.
- You can press **2ND ENTER** over and over again to cycle backwards through all the computations you have ever done.
- Know where the $\sqrt{\ }$, π, and $\wedge$ buttons are so you can reach them quickly.
- Change a decimal to a fraction by pressing **MATH ENTER ENTER**.
- Press the **MATH** button - in the first menu that appears you can take cube roots and nth roots for any n.
- Know how to use the **SIN**, **COS** and **TAN** buttons as well as **SIN^{-1}**, **COS^{-1}** and **TAN^{-1}**.

You may find the following graphing tools useful.

- Press the **Y=** button to enter a function, and then hit **ZOOM 6** to graph it in a standard window.
- Practice using the **WINDOW** button to adjust the viewing window of your graph.
- Practice using the **TRACE** button to move along the graph and look at some of the points plotted.
- Pressing **2ND TRACE** (which is really **CALC**) will bring up a menu of useful items. For example, selecting **ZERO** will tell you where the graph hits the x-axis, or equivalently where the function is zero. Selecting **MINIMUM** or **MAXIMUM** can find the vertex of a parabola. Selecting **INTERSECT** will find the point of intersection of 2 graphs.

11. Grid your answers correctly

The computer only grades what you have marked in the bubbles. The space above the bubbles is just for your convenience, and to help you do your bubbling correctly.

Never mark more than one circle in a column or the problem will automatically be marked wrong. You do not need to use all four columns. If you do not use a column just leave it blank.

The symbols that you can grid in are the digits 0 through 9, a decimal point, and a division symbol for fractions. Note that there is no negative symbol. So answers to grid-ins *cannot* be negative. Also, there are only four slots, so you cannot get an answer such as 52,326.

Sometimes there is more than one correct answer to a grid-in question. Simply choose one of them to grid-in. *Never* try to fit more than one answer into the grid.

If your answer is a whole number such as 2451 or a decimal that only requires four or less slots such as 2.36, then simply enter the number starting at any column. The two examples just written must be started in the first column, but the number 16 can be entered starting in column 1, 2 or 3.

Note that there is no zero in column 1, so if your answer is 0 it must be gridded into column 2, 3 or 4.

Fractions can be gridded in any form as long as there are enough slots. The fraction 2/100 must be reduced to 1/50 simply because the first representation will not fit in the grid.

Fractions can also be converted to decimals before being gridded in. If a decimal cannot fit in the grid, then you can simply *truncate* it to fit. But you must use every slot in this case. For example, the decimal .167777777... can be gridded as .167, but .16 or .17 would both be marked wrong.

Instead of truncating decimals you can also *round* them. For example, the decimal above could be gridded as .168. Truncating is preferred because there is no thinking involved and you are less likely to make a careless error.

Here are three ways to grid in the number 8/9.

Never grid-in mixed numerals. If your answer is $2\frac{1}{4}$, and you grid in the mixed numeral $2\frac{1}{4}$, then this will be read as 21/4 and will be marked wrong. You must either grid in the decimal 2.25 or the improper fraction 9/4.

Here are two ways to grid in the mixed numeral $1\frac{1}{2}$ correctly.

PROBLEMS BY LEVEL AND TOPIC WITH FULLY EXPLAINED SOLUTIONS

Note: An asterisk (*) before a question indicates that a calculator is required. An asterisk (*) before a solution indicates that the quickest solution is being given.

LEVEL 1: HEART OF ALGEBRA

1. An author has a book available in paperback and digital formats. The author earns $2.47 on each paperback sale and $3.56 for each digital download. Which of the following expressions represents the amount, in dollars, that the author earns if p paperbacks are sold and d digital books are downloaded?

   (A) $2.47p + 3.56d$
   (B) $2.47p - 3.56d$
   (C) $3.56p + 2.47d$
   (D) $3.56p - 2.47d$

* **Algebraic solution:** The total amount the author earns from paperback sales, in dollars, is $2.47p$ and the total amount the author earns in digital downloads is $3.56d$. So all together the total amount that the author earns is $2.47p + 3.56d$, choice A.

Notes: (1) If 1 paperback is sold, the author earns 2.47 dollars.

If 2 paperbacks are sold, the author earns $2.47 \cdot 2 = 4.94$ dollars.

If 3 paperbacks are sold, the author earns $2.47 \cdot 3 = 7.41$ dollars.

Following this pattern, we see that if p paperbacks are sold, the author earns $2.47p$ dollars.

(2) A similar analysis to what was done in Note (1) shows that if d digital books are downloaded, the author earns $3.56d$ dollars. Try plugging in different values for d, starting at $d = 1$, so that you can see this for yourself.

Solution by picking numbers: Let's suppose that 10 paperbacks were sold and the book was downloaded 2 times. Then we have $p = 10$ and $d = 2$.

The total amount the author earns from paperback sales, in dollars, is $2.47 \cdot 10 = 24.70$. The total amount the author earns from digital downloads is $3.56 \cdot 2 = 7.12$ So the total the author earns, in dollars, is $24.70 + 7.12 = \mathbf{31.82}$.

Put a nice big dark circle around $\mathbf{31.82}$ so you can find it easier later. We now substitute $p = 10$ and $d = 2$ into each answer choice:

(A) $24.7 + 7.12 = 31.82$
(B) $24.7 - 7.12 = 17.58$
(C) $35.6 + 4.94 = 40.54$
(D) $35.6 - 4.94 = 30.66$

Since B, C and D each came out incorrect, the answer is choice A.

Important note: A is **not** the correct answer simply because it is equal to 31.82. It is correct because all three of the other choices are **not** 31.82. **You absolutely must check all four choices!**

Remark: All of the above computations can be done in a single step with your calculator (if a calculator is allowed for this problem).

Notes about picking numbers: (1) Observe that we picked a different number for each variable. We are less likely to get more than one answer choice to come out to the correct answer this way.

(2) We picked numbers that were simple, but not too simple. In general we might want to avoid 0 and 1 because more than one choice is likely to come out correct with these choices. 2 and 3 would normally be good choices (especially if a calculator is allowed). In this case 10 is particularly nice because multiplying by 10 is very easy (just move the decimal point to the right one unit).

(3) When using the strategy of picking numbers, it is very important that we check every answer choice. It is possible for more than one choice to come out to the correct answer. We would then need to pick new numbers to try to eliminate all but one choice.

2.   If $5b + 3 < 18$, which of the following CANNOT be the value of b ?

(A) 0
(B) 1
(C) 2
(D) 3

Solution by starting with choice D: We start with choice D and substitute 3 in for b in the given inequality.

$$5b + 3 < 18$$
$$5(3) + 3 < 18$$
$$15 + 3 < 18$$
$$18 < 18$$

Since this is FALSE, the answer is choice D.

Notes: (1) A basic SAT math strategy that every student should know is "plugging in the answer choices." To use this strategy, we simply try out each answer choice until we find the one that "works." If we have no other information we would generally start with choice B or C as our first guess. In this particular problem, a little thought should convince you that the answer must be one of the extreme values.

(2) If we were to try choice C first, then the left hand side of the inequality gives us $5(2) + 3 = 10 + 3 = 13$. Since $13 < 18$ is true, we see that 2 CAN be a solution. This computation not only allows us to eliminate choice C as an answer, but choices A and B as well.

* (3) A moment's thought tells us that we are looking for a number that is too big. So the largest number given must be the answer. Using this reasoning, we can actually solve this problem without doing a single computation.

Algebraic solution:

$$5b + 3 < 18$$
$$5b < 15$$
$$b < 3$$

Thus, the answer is choice D.

Notes: (1) We get from the first inequality to the second by subtracting 3 from each side: $(5b + 3) - 3 = 5b$ and $18 - 3 = 15$

(2) We get from the second inequality to the third inequality by dividing each side by 5: $\frac{5b}{5} = b$ and $\frac{15}{5} = 3$.

3. Perfect Floors Carpeting is hired to lay down carpet in k rooms of equal size. Perfect Floor's fee can be calculated by the expression $kA\ell w$, where k is the number of rooms, A is the cost per square foot of the carpet in dollars, ℓ is the length of each room in feet, and w is the width of each room in feet. If the customer chooses to use more expensive material for the carpet, which of the factors in the expression would change?

(A) k
(B) A
(C) ℓ
(D) w

* A is the cost per square foot of the carpet in dollars. If a customer chooses to use more expensive carpeting material, then A will increase. So the answer is B.

Notes: (1) k would increase if the customer decides to have more rooms carpeted (the rooms would need to be of equal size), and k would decrease if the customer decided to carpet less rooms.

(2) ℓ would increase if the customer decided to carpet rooms that were longer, and ℓ would decrease if the customer decided to carpet rooms that were shorter.

(3) w would increase if the customer decided to carpet rooms that were wider, and w would decrease if the customer decided to carpet rooms that were less wide.

4. For $i = \sqrt{-1}$, the sum $(-2 + 7i) + (-3 - 4i)$ is equal to

(A) $-5 - 11i$
(B) $-5 + 3i$
(C) $\ 1 - 11i$
(D) $\ 1 + 3i$

* $(-2 + 7i) + (-3 - 4i) = (-2 - 3) + (7 - 4)i = -5 + 3i$, choice B.

Notes: (1) The numbers $-2 + 7i$ and $-3 - 4i$ are **complex numbers**. In general, a complex number has the form $a + bi$, where a and b are real numbers and $i = \sqrt{-1}$.

a is called the **real part** of the complex number and b is called the **imaginary part** of the complex number.

21

(2) We add two complex numbers simply by adding their real parts, and then adding their imaginary parts.

$$(a + bi) + (c + di) = (a + c) + (b + d)i$$

In this question, we have $a = -2$, $b = 7$, $c = -3$, and $d = -4$.

5.   If $c > 0$ and $5c^2 - 45 = 0$, what is the value of c ?

* Algebraic solution: We add 45 to each side of the equation to get $5c^2 = 45$. We then divide each side of this last equation by 5 to get $c^2 = \frac{45}{5} = 9$. Since $3^2 = 9$ and $3 > 0$, the answer is **3**.

Notes: (1) We can also begin by factoring and dividing each side of the given equation by 5.

$$5(c^2 - 9) = 0$$
$$c^2 - 9 = 0$$

We can then add 9 to each side of the equation to get $c^2 = 9$, and then proceed as in the solution above to get $c = 3$.

(2) The equation $c^2 = 9$ has two solution $c = \pm 3$. We reject the negative solution because we are given $c > 0$.

(3) As an alternative to the method in Note (1), we can factor $c^2 - 9$ as the difference of two squares: $c^2 - 9 = (c - 3)(c + 3)$, and then set each factor equal to 0 to get $c - 3 = 0$ or $c + 3 = 0$. From these last two equations we get $c = 3$ or $c = -3$. Once again, since we are given $c > 0$, we choose $c = 3$.

(4) We can also just plug guesses for c in to the left hand side of the equation until we get 0. We will eventually see that

$$5(3)^2 - 45 = 5 \cdot 9 - 45 = 45 - 45 = 0.$$

So the answer is 3.

6.   If $2\left(\frac{x-3}{5}\right) = b$ and $b = 4$, what is the value of x ?

* Algebraic solution: Replacing b with 4 gives us $2\left(\frac{x-3}{5}\right) = 4$. We multiply each side of the equation by $\frac{5}{2}$ to get $x - 3 = 4 \cdot \frac{5}{2} = 10$. Finally, we add 3 to each side of this last equation to get $x = 10 + 3 = \mathbf{13}$.

Notes: (1) $2\left(\frac{x-3}{5}\right) = \frac{2}{5}(x-3)$. To get rid of the $\frac{2}{5}$, we multiply by its reciprocal (which is $\frac{5}{2}$).

(2) As an alternative to multiplying by $\frac{5}{2}$, we can first divide each side of the equation by 2, and then multiply each side of the resulting equation by 5. Here are the steps in detail:

$$2\left(\frac{x-3}{5}\right) = 4$$

$$\frac{2}{2}\left(\frac{x-3}{5}\right) = \frac{4}{2}$$

$$\frac{x-3}{5} = 2$$

$$5\left(\frac{x-3}{5}\right) = 2 \cdot 5$$

$$x - 3 = 10$$

(3) It's nice to practice solving these equations in your head informally. See if you can understand and then emulate the following reasoning.

What do we multiply 2 by to get 4? Well, 2 times 2 is 4. So $\frac{x-3}{5}$ must be 2. Now, what divided by 5 is 2. Well, 10 divided by 5 is 2. So $x - 3$ must be 10. Finally, what number minus 3 is 10? Well, 13 minus 3 is 10. So x must be 13.

7.   If $7x - 3 = 17$, what is the value of $14x - 5$?

* Algebraic solution: We add 3 to each side of the given equation to get $7x = 17 + 3$, or $7x = 20$. We now multiply each side of this last equation by 2 to get $14x = 40$. Finally, we subtract 5 from each side of this last equation to get $14x - 5 = 40 - 5 = \mathbf{35}$.

Notes: (1) We did *not* need to find x to solve this problem. Since the expression we are trying to find has $14x$ as one of its terms, it is more efficient to multiply $7x$ by 2, than it is to solve the original equation for x and then multiply by 14.

(2) If you didn't notice that you could change $7x$ into $14x$ by multiplying by 2, then the problem could be solved as follows:

$$7x - 3 = 17$$
$$7x = 20$$
$$x = \frac{20}{7}$$
$$14x = \frac{20}{7} \cdot 14$$
$$14x = 20 \cdot 2$$
$$14x = 40$$
$$14x - 5 = 40 - 5$$
$$14x - 5 = 35$$

8.   Last month Josephine worked 7 less hours than Maria. If they worked a combined total of 137 hours, how many hours did Maria work that month?

* Algebraic solution: Let x be the number of hours Maria worked. Then Josephine worked $x - 7$ hours, and we have $x + (x - 7) = 137$. Therefore, $2x - 7 = 137$, and so $2x = 137 + 7 = 144$. So the number of hours that Maria worked is $x = \frac{144}{2} = \textbf{72.}$

Note: This problem can also be solved by guessing. I leave the details of this solution to the reader.

LEVEL 1: GEOMETRY AND TRIG

9.   What is the diameter of a circle whose area is 16π?

(A) 4
(B) 8
(C) 16
(D) 8π

Solution by starting with choice C: The area of a circle is $A = \pi r^2$. Let's start with choice C as our first guess. If $d = 16$, then $r = 8$, and so we have $A = \pi \cdot 8^2 = \pi \cdot 64 = 64\pi$. Since this is too big we can eliminate choices C and D.

Let's try choice B next. If $d = 8$, then $r = 4$, and so $A = \pi \cdot 4^2 = 16\pi$. This is correct, and so the answer is choice B.

24

Notes: (1) A **circle** is a two-dimensional geometric figure formed of a curved line surrounding a center point, every point of the line being an equal distance from the center point. This distance is called the **radius** of the circle. The **diameter** of a circle is the distance between any two points on the circle that pass through the center of the circle.

(2) The diameter of a circle is twice the radius of the circle.

$$d = 2r$$

* Algebraic solution: We use the area formula $A = \pi r^2$, and substitute 16π in for A.

$$A = \pi r^2$$
$$16\pi = \pi r^2$$
$$16 = r^2$$
$$4 = r$$

Now, the diameter of a circle is twice the radius, and so we have $d = 2r = 2 \cdot 4 = 8$, choice B.

Note: The equation $r^2 = 16$ would normally have two solutions:

$$r = 4 \text{ and } r = -4.$$

But the radius of a circle must be positive, and so we reject -4.

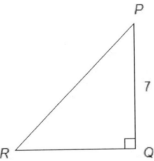

10. In the isosceles right triangle above, $PQ = 7$. What is the length, in inches, of $\overline{PR}$?

(A) $7\sqrt{2}$
(B) $\sqrt{14}$
(C) 14
(D) 7

Solution by the Pythagorean Theorem: Since the triangle is isosceles, $RQ = PQ = 7$. By the Pythagorean Theorem, we have

$$PR^2 = 7^2 + 7^2 = 49 + 49 = 49 \cdot 2.$$

So $PR = \sqrt{49 \cdot 2} = \sqrt{49} \cdot \sqrt{2} = 7\sqrt{2}$, choice A.

Remarks: (1) The Pythagorean Theorem says that if a right triangle has legs of length a and b, and a hypotenuse of length c, then $c^2 = a^2 + b^2$.

(2) The Pythagorean Theorem is one of the formulas given to you in the beginning of each math section.

(3) The equation $PR^2 = 49 \cdot 2$ would normally have two solutions:

$$PR = 7\sqrt{2} \text{ and } PR = -7\sqrt{2}.$$

But the length of a side of a triangle cannot be negative, and so we reject $-7\sqrt{2}$.

(4) A **triangle** is a two-dimensional geometric figure with three sides and three angles. The sum of the degree measures of all three angles of a triangle is $180°$.

(5) A triangle is **isosceles** if it has two sides of equal length. Equivalently, an isosceles triangle has two angles of equal measure.

* Solution using a 45, 45, 90 triangle: An isosceles right triangle is the same as a 45, 45, 90 triangle, and so the hypotenuse has length $PR = 7\sqrt{2}$, choice A.

Note: The following two special triangles are given on the SAT:

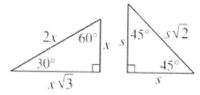

Some students get a bit confused because there are variables in these pictures. We can simplify the pictures if we substitute a 1 in for the variables.

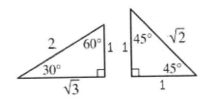

Notice that the sides of the 30, 60, 90 triangle are then 1, 2 and $\sqrt{3}$ and the sides of the 45, 45, 90 triangle are 1, 1 and $\sqrt{2}$. The variables in the first picture above just tell us that if we multiply one of the sides in the second picture by a number, then we have to multiply the other two sides by the same number. For example, instead of 1, 1 and $\sqrt{2}$, we can have 7, 7 and $7\sqrt{2}$ (here $s = 7$), or $\sqrt{2}, \sqrt{2}$, and 2 (here $s = \sqrt{2}$).

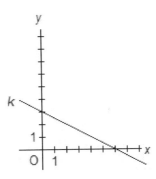

11. What is the equation of line k in the figure above?

(A) $2x + y = 3$

(B) $2x + y = 6$

(C) $x + 2y = 6$

(D) $x + 2y = 12$

Solution by plugging in points: Since the point $(0, 3)$ lies on the line, if we substitute 0 in for x and 3 in for y, we should get a true equation.

(A) $3 = 3$	True
(B) $3 = 6$	False
(C) $6 = 6$	True
(D) $6 = 12$	False

We can eliminate choices B and D because they came out False

27

The point $(6, 0)$ also lies on the line. So if we substitute 6 for x and 0 for y we should also get a true equation.

(A) $12 = 3$ False

(C) $6 = 6$ True

We can eliminate choice A because it came out False. Therefore, the answer is choice C.

* Solution using the slope-intercept form of an equation of a line: Recall that the slope-intercept form for the equation of a line is

$$y = mx + b.$$

$(0, 3)$ is the y-intercept of the point. Thus, $b = 3$. The slope of the given line is $m = \dfrac{\text{rise}}{\text{run}} = \dfrac{-3}{6} = \dfrac{-1}{2}$. Thus, the equation of the line in slope-intercept form is $y = -\dfrac{1}{2}x + 3$.

We multiply each side of this equation by 2 to get $2y = -x + 6$. Finally, we add x to each side of this last equation to get $x + 2y = 6$, choice C.

Notes: (1) To find the slope using the graph we simply note that to get from the y-intercept of the line to the x-intercept of the line we need to move down 3, then right 6.

(2) The answer choices are in **general form**. To change the equation of a line from slope-intercept form to general form we first eliminate all fractions by multiplying each side of the equation by the least common denominator. In this case, that is 2. Here are the steps in detail:

$$y = -\frac{1}{2}x + 3$$
$$2y = 2(-\frac{1}{2}x + 3)$$
$$2y = 2\left(-\frac{1}{2}x\right) + 2(3)$$
$$2y = -x + 6$$

We now simply add x to each side of this last equation to get

$$x + 2y = 6.$$

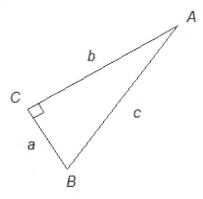

12. In the figure above, what is $\sin A$?

    (A) $\dfrac{c}{b}$

    (B) $\dfrac{a}{b}$

    (C) $\dfrac{a}{c}$

    (D) $\dfrac{b}{a}$

* $\sin A \ = \ \dfrac{\text{OPP}}{\text{HYP}} \ = \ \dfrac{a}{c}$, choice C.

Here is a quick lesson in **right triangle trigonometry** for those of you that have forgotten.

Let's begin by focusing on angle A in the following picture:

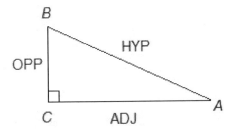

Note that the **hypotenuse** is ALWAYS the side opposite the right angle.

The other two sides of the right triangle, called the **legs**, depend on which angle is chosen. In this picture we chose to focus on angle A. Therefore, the opposite side is BC, and the adjacent side is AC.

29

Now you should simply memorize how to compute the six trig functions:

$$\sin A = \frac{\text{OPP}}{\text{HYP}} \qquad\qquad \csc A = \frac{\text{HYP}}{\text{OPP}}$$

$$\cos A = \frac{\text{ADJ}}{\text{HYP}} \qquad\qquad \sec A = \frac{\text{HYP}}{\text{ADJ}}$$

$$\tan A = \frac{\text{OPP}}{\text{ADJ}} \qquad\qquad \cot A = \frac{\text{ADJ}}{\text{OPP}}$$

Here are a couple of tips to help you remember these:

(1) Many students find it helpful to use the word SOHCAHTOA. You can think of the letters here as representing sin, opp, hyp, cos, adj, hyp, tan, opp, adj.

(2) The three trig functions on the right are the reciprocals of the three trig functions on the left. In other words, you get them by interchanging the numerator and denominator. It's pretty easy to remember that the reciprocal of tangent is cotangent. For the other two, just remember that the "s" goes with the "c" and the "c" goes with the "s." In other words, the reciprocal of sine is cosecant, and the reciprocal of cosine is secant.

To make sure you understand this, compute all six trig functions for each of the angles (except the right angle) in the triangle given in this problem. Please try this yourself before looking at the answers below.

$$\sin A = \frac{a}{c} \qquad \csc A = \frac{c}{a} \qquad \sin B = \frac{b}{c} \qquad \csc B = \frac{c}{b}$$

$$\cos A = \frac{b}{c} \qquad \sec A = \frac{c}{b} \qquad \cos B = \frac{a}{c} \qquad \sec B = \frac{c}{a}$$

$$\tan A = \frac{a}{b} \qquad \cot A = \frac{b}{a} \qquad \tan B = \frac{b}{a} \qquad \cot B = \frac{a}{b}$$

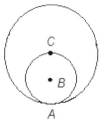

13. In the figure above, A, B, and C lie on the same line. B is the center of the smaller circle, and C is the center of the larger circle. If the diameter of the larger circle is 28, what is the radius of the smaller circle?

Solution by assuming the figure is drawn to scale: We can assume that the figure is drawn to scale.

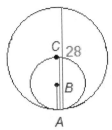

The three lines drawn in the picture above are just there for the purposes of measurement. In practice, you can just use your fingers to measure.

The smallest segment is the radius of the smaller circle. The longest segment is the diameter of the larger circle.

From the picture it is easy to see that the radius of the smaller circle is $\frac{1}{4}$ the diameter of the larger circle. So the answer is $\frac{1}{4} \cdot 28 = $ **7**.

* Geometric solution: Since the radius of a circle is half the diameter, the radius of the larger circle is $\frac{1}{2} \cdot 28 = 14$. This is also the diameter of the smaller circle. Therefore, the radius of the smaller circle is $\frac{1}{2} \cdot 14 = $ **7**.

Note: Figure not drawn to scale.

14.   In right triangle ABC above, what is the length of side AB?

* Solution using the Pythagorean Theorem: We use the Pythagorean Theorem: $c^2 = a^2 + b^2 = 38 + 11 = 49$. Therefore, $AB = c = $ **7**.

Note: See problem 10 for more information on the Pythagorean Theorem.

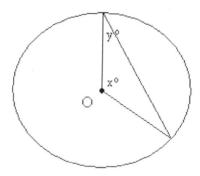

15. In the figure above, if $x = 122$ and O is the center of the circle, what is the value of y ?

* Algebraic solution: Note that the triangle is **isosceles**. In particular, y is equal to the measure of the unlabeled angle. Therefore, we have the following

$$x + y + y = 180$$
$$122 + 2y = 180$$
$$2y = 180 - 122$$
$$2y = 58$$
$$y = \frac{58}{2}$$
$$y = \mathbf{29}$$

Notes: (1) See problem 10 for more information about isosceles triangles.

(2) All radii of a circle are equal. So if two sides of a triangle are radii of a circle, then the triangle must be isosceles.

(3) In an isosceles triangle, angles opposite the two equal sides have equal measure.

16. In the standard (x, y) coordinate plane, what is the slope of the line segment joining the points $(-2, -3)$ and $(6, -1)$?

Solution by drawing a picture: Let's plot the two points.

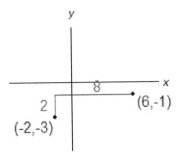

Note that to get from $(-2, -3)$ to $(6, -1)$ we move up 2 and right 8. Therefore, the answer is $2/8 = $ **1/4** or **.25**.

Note: If you cannot see where the 2 and 8 come from visually, then you can formally find the differences:

$$-1 - (-3) = -1 + 3 = 2 \text{ and } 6 - (-2) = 6 + 2 = 8.$$

* Solution using the slope formula: $\frac{-1-(-3)}{6-(-2)} = \frac{-1+3}{6+2} = \frac{2}{8} = $ **1/4** or **.25**.

Notes: (1) The slope of the line passing through the points (x_1, y_1) and (x_2, y_2) is

$$\text{Slope} = m = \frac{\text{rise}}{\text{run}} = \frac{y_2 - y_1}{x_2 - x_1}$$

Here, the points are $(x_1, y_1) = (-2, -3)$ and $(x_2, y_2) = (6, -1)$.

(2) Lines with **positive slope** have graphs that go upwards from left to right.

Lines with **negative slope** have graphs that go downwards from left to right.

Horizontal lines have **zero slope**.

Vertical lines have **no slope** (or **infinite slope** or **undefined slope**).

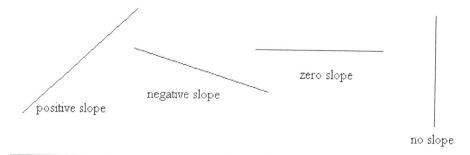

zero slope

negative slope

positive slope

no slope

LEVEL 1: PASSPORT TO ADVANCED MATH

$$3x(y + 2z)$$

17. Which of the following is equivalent to the expression above?

    (A) $xy + 5xz$
    (B) $3xy + 5xz$
    (C) $3xy + 2z$
    (D) $3xy + 6xz$

* Solution using the distributive property:

$$3x(y + 2z) = 3x \cdot y + 3x \cdot 2z = 3xy + 6xz$$

So the answer is choice D.

Notes: (1) The **distributive property** says that for all real numbers a, b, and c

$$a(b + c) = ab + ac$$

More specifically, this property says that the operation of multiplication distributes over addition. The distributive property is very important as it allows us to multiply and factor algebraic expressions.

In this problem, $a = 3x$, $b = y$, and $c = 2z$.

(2) $3x \cdot 2z = 3 \cdot 2 \cdot x \cdot z = 6xz$. Similarly, $3x \cdot y = 3xy$.

Solution by picking numbers: Let's choose values for x, y, and z, say $x = 2$, $y = 3$, and $z = 4$. Then

$$3x(y + 2z) = 3 \cdot 2(3 + 2 \cdot 4) = 6(3 + 8) = 6 \cdot 11 = \mathbf{66}.$$

Put a nice big, dark circle around this number so that you can find it easily later. We now substitute the numbers that we chose into each answer choice.

(A) $2 * 3 + 5 * 2 * 4 = 6 + 40 = 64$
(B) $3 * 2 * 3 + 5 * 2 * 4 = 18 + 40 = 58$
(C) $3 * 2 * 3 + 2 * 4 = 18 + 8 = 26$
(D) $3 * 2 * 3 + 6 * 2 * 4 = 18 + 48 = 66$

Since A, B and C are incorrect we can eliminate them. Therefore, the answer is choice D.

Notes: (1) D is **not** the correct answer simply because it is equal to 66. It is correct because all 3 of the other choices are **not** 66.

(2) See problem 1 for more information on picking numbers.

18. If $f(x) = 5(x - 2) + 3$, which of the following is equivalent to $f(x)$?

(A) $3 - 10x$
(B) $5x - 7$
(C) $5x - 5$
(D) $5x + 1$

* Solution using the distributive property: We have

$$5(x - 2) + 3 = 5x - 10 + 3 = 5x - 7$$

So $f(x) = 5x - 7$, choice B.

Notes: (1) The **distributive property** says that if a, b, and c are real numbers, then

$$a(b + c) = ab + ac.$$

In this question, $a = 5$, $b = x$, and $c = -2$.

So we have $5(x - 2) = 5(x + (-2)) = 5x + 5(-2) = 5x - 10$.

(2) A common mistake would be to write $5(x - 2) = 5x - 2$. This would lead to $5(x - 2) + 3 = 5x - 2 + 3 = 5x + 1$. This is choice D which is **wrong!**

Solution by picking a number: Let's choose a value for x, say $x = 2$. It then follows that $f(x) = f(2) = 5(2 - 2) + 3 = 5 \cdot 0 + 3 = 3$. Put a nice, big, dark circle around this number so that you can find it easily later. We now substitute $x = 2$ into each answer choice.

(A) $3 - 10x = 3 - 10 \cdot 2 = 3 - 20 = -17$
(B) $5x - 7 = 5 \cdot 2 - 7 = 10 - 7 = 3$
(C) $5x - 5 = 5 \cdot 2 - 5 = 10 - 5 = 5$
(D) $5x + 1 = 5 \cdot 2 + 1 = 10 + 1 = 11$

We now compare each of these numbers to the number that we put a nice big, dark circle around. Since A, C and D are incorrect we can eliminate them. Therefore, the answer is choice B.

Important note: B is **not** the correct answer simply because it is equal to 3. It is correct because all three of the other choices are **not** 3. **You absolutely must check all four choices!**

19. Which of the following graphs is the graph of a function?

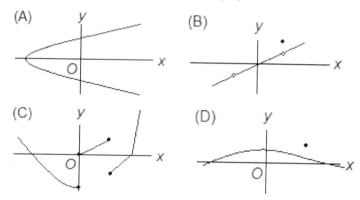

* **Direct solution:** Only choice B passes the **vertical line test**. In other words, any vertical line will hit the graph *at most* once. The answer is B.

Notes: (1) Observe how the following vertical line hits the graph *only* once:

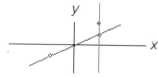

Only the solid dot is a point on the graph. The open circle indicates that there is no point there.

36

(2) There is also a vertical line that does not hit the graph at all. This is okay – a vertical line has to hit the graph *at most* once. This means one time *or* zero times.

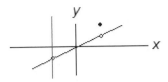

Solution by process of elimination: To eliminate an answer choice, it suffices to draw a vertical line that hits the graph more than once.

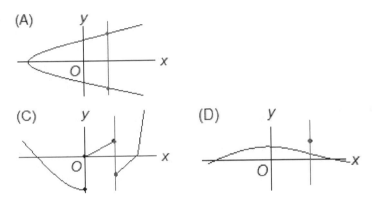

This eliminates choices A, C, and D. So the answer is B.

20. If $3k^2 - 33 = 12 - 2k^2$, what are all possible values of k ?

    (A) 3 only
    (B) -3 only
    (C) 0 only
    (D) 3 and -3 only

Solution by plugging in the answer choices: According to the answer choices we need only check 0, 3, and -3.

$k = 0$: $3(0)^2 - 33 = 12 - 2(0)^2$ $-33 = 12$ False

$k = 3$: $3(3)^2 - 33 = 12 - 2(3)^2$ $-6 = -6$ True

$k = -3$: $3(-3)^2 - 33 = 12 - 2(-3)^2$ $-6 = -6$ True

So the answer is choice D.

Notes: (1) Since all powers of k in the given equation are even, 2 and -2 must give the same answer. So we didn't really need to check -2.

(2) Observe that when performing the computations above, the proper order of operations was followed. Exponentiation was done first, followed by multiplication, and then subtraction was done last.

For example, we have $3(3)^2 - 33 = 3 \cdot 9 - 33 = 27 - 33 = -6$ and $12 - 2(3)^2 = 12 - 2 \cdot 9 = 12 - 18 = -6$.

Order of Operations: Here is a quick review of order of operations.

PEMDAS	
P	Parentheses
E	Exponentiation
M	Multiplication
D	Division
A	Addition
S	Subtraction

Note that multiplication and division have the same priority, and addition and subtraction have the same priority.

* Algebraic solution: We add $2k^2$ to each side of the given equation to get $5k^2 - 33 = 12$. We then add 33 to get $5k^2 = 12 + 33 = 45$. Dividing each side of this last equation by 5 gives $k^2 = \frac{45}{5} = 9$. We now use the **square root property** to get $k = \pm 3$. So the answer is choice D.

Notes: (1) The equation $k^2 = 9$ has two solutions: $k = 3$ and $k = -3$. A common mistake is to forget about the negative solution.

(2) The **square root property** says that if $x^2 = c$, then $x = \pm\sqrt{c}$.

This is different from taking the positive square root of a number. For example, $\sqrt{9} = 3$, while the equation $x^2 = 9$ has two solutions $x = \pm 3$.

(3) Another way to solve the equation $k^2 = 9$ is to subtract 9 from each side of the equation, and then factor the difference of two squares as follows:

$$k^2 - 9 = 0$$
$$(k - 3)(k + 3) = 0$$

We now set each factor equal to 0 to get $k - 3 = 0$ or $k + 3 = 0$. Thus, $k = 3$ or $k = -3$.

38

21. A triangle has area A, base b, and height h. Which of the following represents b in terms of A and h ?

    (A) $b = \dfrac{A}{2h}$

    (B) $b = \dfrac{A}{h}$

    (C) $b = \dfrac{2A}{h}$

    (D) $b = \dfrac{\sqrt{A}}{h}$

* Algebraic solution: The area of a triangle is $A = \frac{1}{2}bh$. Multiplying each side of this equation by 2 gives $bh = 2A$. Dividing each side of this last equation by h gives $b = \frac{2A}{h}$, choice C.

Note: We can solve the equation $A = \frac{1}{2}bh$ for b in a single step by multiplying each side of the equation by $\frac{2}{h}$.

Solution by picking numbers: Let's let $b = 2$ and $h = 3$, so that $A = 3$. Put a nice big dark circle around **2** so you can find it easier later. We now substitute $A = 3$ and $h = 3$ into each answer choice:

    (A) $w = \dfrac{3}{2\cdot3} = \dfrac{1}{2} = 0.5$

    (B) $w = \dfrac{3}{3} = 1$

    (C) $w = \dfrac{2\cdot3}{3} = 2$

    (D) $w = \dfrac{\sqrt{3}}{3}$

Since A, B, and D each came out incorrect, the answer is choice C.

Important note: C is **not** the correct answer simply because it is equal to 3. It is correct because all three of the other choices are **not** 3. **You absolutely must check all four choices!**

Remark: All of the above computations can be done in a single step with your calculator (if a calculator is allowed for this problem).

$$f(x) = 2x^3 - 5$$
$$g(x) = \frac{1}{2}x + 1$$

22. The functions f and g are defined above. What is the value of $g(4) - f(1)$?

* $g(4) = \frac{1}{2}(4) + 1 = 2 + 1 = 3$.

$f(1) = 2 \cdot 1^3 - 5 = 2 \cdot 1 - 5 = 2 - 5 = -3$.

Therefore, $g(4) - f(1) = 3 - (-3) = 3 + 3 = \mathbf{6}$.

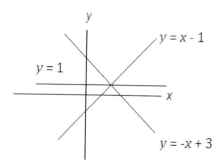

23. Three equations and their graphs in the xy-plane are shown above. How many solutions does the system consisting of those three equations have?

* From the graphs we see that this system has one solution. It is the point of intersection of all 3 graphs. The answer is **1**.

Notes: (1) The figure shows three graphs in the xy-plane. These are the graphs of the following system of equations:

$$y = \quad x - 1$$
$$y = -x + 3$$
$$y = \qquad 1$$

(2) To find the point of intersection of the three graphs, first observe that all three points must have y-coordinate 1 (because $y = 1$ is one of the equations). We can now substitute $y = 1$ into either of the other two equations to find x. For example, $1 = x - 1$ implies that $x = 2$. So the only solution to the given system is $(2, 1)$.

(3) Let's just check that the point $(2, 1)$ is also on the graph of the equation $y = -x + 3$. If we substitute 1 for x, we get $y = -1 + 3 = 2$.

40

24. If $y = kx$ and $y = 7$ when $x = 11$, then what is y when $x = 33$?

Algebraic solution: We are given that $y = 7$ when $x = 11$, so $7 = k(11)$, or $k = \frac{7}{11}$. Therefore $y = \frac{7x}{11}$. When $x = 33$, we have $y = \frac{7(33)}{11} = \mathbf{21}$.

Solution using direct variation: Since $y = kx$, y varies directly as x, and so $\frac{y}{x}$ is a constant. So we get the following ratio: $\frac{7}{11} = \frac{y}{33}$. Cross multiplying gives $7 \cdot 33 = 11y$, so that $y = \frac{7 \cdot 33}{11} = \mathbf{21}$.

Graphical solution: The graph of $y = f(x)$ is a line passing through the points $(0, 0)$ and $(11, 7)$ The slope of this line is $\frac{7 - 0}{11 - 0} = \frac{7}{11}$. Writing the equation of the line in slope-intercept form we have $y = \frac{7}{11}x$. As in solution 1, when $x = 33$, we have $y = \frac{7(33)}{11} = \mathbf{21}$.

* Quick solution: To get from $x = 11$ to $x = 33$ we multiply x by 3. So we have to also multiply y by 3. We get $3(7) = \mathbf{21}$.

Note: The following are all equivalent ways of saying the same thing:

(1) y varies directly as x.
(2) y is directly proportional to x.
(3) $y = kx$ for some constant k.
(4) $\frac{y}{x}$ is constant.
(5) The graph of $y = f(x)$ is a nonvertical line through the origin.

LEVEL 1: PROBLEM SOLVING AND DATA

25. A dentist sees 3 patients in 45 minutes. At this rate, how many patients would the dentist see in 3 <u>hours</u>?

(A) 9
(B) 12
(C) 14
(D) 15

Solution by setting up a ratio: We identify 2 key words. Let's choose "patients" and "minutes."

patients	3	x
minutes	45	180

Choose the words that are most helpful to you. Notice that we wrote in the number of patients next to the word patients, and the number of minutes next to the word minutes. Also notice that the number 45 is written under the number 3 because the dentist can see 3 patients in 45 minutes. Similarly, the number 180 is written under the unknown quantity x because we are trying to find out how many patients the dentist can see in 180 minutes (= 3 hours).

We now find x by cross multiplying and dividing.

$$\frac{3}{45} = \frac{x}{180}$$
$$45x = 3 \cdot 180$$
$$x = \frac{3 \cdot 180}{45} = 12$$

So the answer is choice B.

Notes: (1) At first glance it might seem to make more sense to choose "hours" as our second key word, but choosing the word "minutes" here will allow us to avoid having to work with fractions or decimals.

(2) There are 60 minutes in an hour. It follows that 3 hours is equal to $3 \cdot 60 = 180$ minutes.

(3) If we are not allowed to use a calculator for this problem, then a quick way to compute $\frac{3 \cdot 180}{45}$ is to first divide 180 by 45 to get 4. We can do this quickly in our head by counting how many 45's are in 180 (45, 90, 135, 180 – indeed there are 4). So we have

$$\frac{3 \cdot 180}{45} = 3 \cdot 4 = 12.$$

(4) If we choose to work in hours instead of minutes, then our initial setup would look as follows:

patients	3	x
hours	.75	3

Once again, we can find x by cross multiplying and dividing.

$$\frac{3}{.75} = \frac{x}{3}$$
$$.75x = 3 \cdot 3$$
$$x = \frac{3 \cdot 3}{.75} = 12$$

This gives us choice B.

* Mental math: 3 patients in 45 minutes is equivalent to 1 patient in 15 minutes. This is equivalent to 4 patients per hour. So in 3 hours the dentist will see $3 \cdot 4 = 12$ patients, choice B.

Questions 26 - 27 refer to the following information.

Favorite Animals

	Dog	Cat	Elephant	Monkey	Lion	Total
Fresh	82	17	20	36	18	173
Soph	51	46	5	50	6	158
Jun	24	30	63	22	30	169
Total	157	93	88	108	54	500

The table above lists the results of a survey of a random sample of 500 high school freshman, sophomores and juniors. Each student selected one animal that was his or her favorite.

26. How many sophomores selected the dog, cat, or lion as their favorite animal?

   (A) 84
   (B) 103
   (C) 117
   (D) 304

* We make sure to look at the row labeled "Soph" and we observe that 51 sophomores selected the dog, 46 sophomores selected the cat, and 6 sophomores selected the lion. So the number of sophomores that selected the dog, cat, or lion is $51 + 46 + 6 = 103$, choice B.

27. ***** What is the percentage of the 500 students that selected the elephant as their favorite animal?

   (A) 1%
   (B) 4%
   (C) 12.6%
   (D) 17.6%

* The total number of students is 500, and the number of these students that selected the elephant as their favorite animal is 88. So the desired percentage is $\frac{88}{500} \times 100 = 17.6\%$, choice D.

Notes: (1) To compute a percentage, use the simple formula

$$Percentage = \frac{Part}{Whole} \times 100$$

In this problem the *Part* is 88 and the *Whole* is 500.

(2) Alternatively we can simply divide the *Part* by the *Whole* and then change the resulting decimal to a percent by moving the decimal point to the right two places.

$$\frac{Part}{Whole} = \frac{88}{500} = 0.176 = 17.6\%$$

28. A tracker was implanted inside a bald eagle's wing, and its flight speed was monitored over a period of 2 hours. The data are graphed on the set of axes below with the time elapsed on the x-axis and the flight speed of the eagle on the y-axis. On which interval is the eagle's flight speed strictly decreasing then strictly increasing?

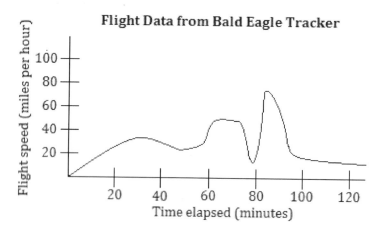

(A) Between 0 and 40 minutes
(B) Between 50 and 60 minutes
(C) Between 75 and 85 minutes
(D) Between 90 and 120 minutes

44

* We are looking for the graph to go down and then up as we move from left to right. This happens between 75 and 85 minutes, choice C.

Notes: (1) Let's isolate the part of the graph between 75 and 85 minutes.

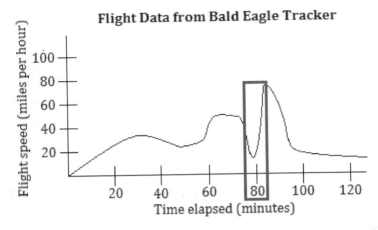

Notice how in the boxed portion, the graph goes down, and then up, as we move from left to right.

(2) Between 0 and 40 minutes, the eagle's flight speed is strictly increasing then strictly decreasing.

(3) Between 50 and 60 minutes, the eagle's flight speed is strictly increasing.

(4) Between 90 and 120 minutes, the eagle's flight speed is strictly decreasing.

29. A data analyst was interested in the mean height of women in a small town. He randomly measured the heights of 200 women in that town, and found that the mean height of these women was 61 inches, and the margin of error for this estimate was 3 inches. The data analyst would like to repeat the procedure and attempt to reduce the margin of error. Which of the following samples would most likely result in a smaller margin of error for the estimated mean height of women in that same town?

    (A) 100 randomly selected people from the same town.
    (B) 100 randomly selected women from the same town.
    (C) 400 randomly selected people from the same town.
    (D) 400 randomly selected women from the same town.

45

* Increasing the sample size while keeping the population the same will most likely decrease the margin of error. So the answer is choice D.

Notes: (1) Decreasing the sample size will increase the margin of error. This allows us to eliminate choices A and B.

(2) The original sample consisted of only women. If we were to allow the second sample to include all people (including men), then we have changed the population. We cannot predict what impact this would have on the mean and margin of error. This allows us to eliminate choice C.

30. A lottery paid out a total of $6000 to players with winning tickets. Some winners received $500 and other winners received $1500. If at least one winner was paid $500 and at least one winner was paid $1500, what is one possible number of $1500 payouts?

* We subtract $500 and $1500 from the $6000 total to get $4000 remaining. Since 4000 is divisible by 500, it's possible that all of the remaining winners were paid $500. It follows that one possible number of $1500 payouts is **1**.

Notes: (1) The number of $1500 payouts can also be **2**, because if we subtract $2 \cdot 1500 = 3000$ from 6000, we get $6000 - 3000 = 3000$, and 3000 is divisible by 500.

Similarly, the number of $1500 payouts can be **3**, because if we subtract $3 \cdot 1500 = 4500$ from 6000, we get $6000 - 4500 = 1500$, and 1500 is divisible by 500.

(2) A complete list of the possible number of $1500 payouts is **1**, **2**, and **3**.

4 won't work because $4 \cdot 1500 = 6000$, and there would be no money left for the requirement of at least one $500 payout.

31. * A traffic sign on an expressway says that a driver must drive at least 45 miles per hour and at most 65 miles per hour. What is a possible amount of time, in hours, that it could take a driver to drive 585 miles, assuming that the driver obeys the traffic sign and does not make any stops?

* $585/65 = 9$ and $585 / 45 = 13$. So we can grid in any number between 9 and 13, inclusive.

Notes: (1) We can use the formula $d = rt$ (distance = rate × time). In this problem, it's easiest to use the formula in the form $t = \frac{d}{r}$.

(2) If the driver travels the whole 585 miles at 45 miles per hour, then the amount of time is $\frac{585}{45} = \textbf{13}$ hours.

(3) If the driver travels the whole 585 miles at 65 miles per hour, then the amount of time is $\frac{585}{65} = \textbf{9}$ hours.

(4) The driver may drive at a speed between 45 and 65 miles per hour, and he may change speed as he drives. This is why we can choose other values between 9 and 13 for the answer if we wish.

32. At a pet store 3 goldfish are selected at random from each group of 20. At this rate, how many goldfish will be selected in total if the pet store has 800 goldfish?

Solution by setting up a ratio: We identify 2 key words. Let's choose "selected" and "group."

$$
\begin{array}{lccc}
\text{selected} & 3 & x \\
\text{group} & 20 & 800
\end{array}
$$

We now find x by cross multiplying and dividing.

$$\frac{3}{20} = \frac{x}{800}$$
$$20x = 3 \cdot 800$$
$$x = \frac{3 \cdot 800}{20} = 3 \cdot 40 = \textbf{120}.$$

* Quick solution: $\frac{800}{20} \cdot 3 = 40 \cdot 3 = \textbf{120}$.

Notes: (1) There are 800 goldfish in total, and there are 20 in each group. So dividing 800 by 20 gives us the number of groups.

$$\frac{800}{20} = 40 \text{ groups}$$

(2) Since 3 goldfish are selected from each group, and there are 40 groups, the total number of goldfish selected is $40 \cdot 3 = 120$.

LEVEL 2: HEART OF ALGEBRA

33. If $\frac{x}{3y} = 2$, what is the value of $\frac{12y}{x}$?

      (A) 1
      (B) 2
      (C) 3
      (D) 4

Solution by picking numbers: Let's choose values for x and y, say $x = 6$ and $y = 1$ (note that $\frac{6}{3 \cdot 1} = 2$). We then have $\frac{12y}{x} = \frac{12 \cdot 1}{6} = 2$, choice B.

Note: We can choose any values for x and y that make the given equation true. As another example, we could have chosen $x = 12$ and $y = 2$.

* Algebraic solution: We have $\frac{x}{y} = 2 \cdot 3 = 6$, so that $\frac{y}{x} = \frac{1}{6}$. We multiply each side of this last equation by 12 to get $\frac{12y}{x} = 12 \cdot \frac{1}{6} = 2$, choice B.

Notes: (1) We multiplied the given equation by 3 to get the first equation in this solution.

$$3 \cdot \frac{x}{3y} = 3 \cdot 2$$
$$\frac{3}{1} \cdot \frac{x}{3y} = 6$$
$$\frac{x}{y} = 6$$

(2) We then take the reciprocal of each side of this last equation. It may help to rewrite 6 as $\frac{6}{1}$.

$$\frac{x}{y} = \frac{6}{1}$$
$$\frac{y}{x} = \frac{1}{6}$$

(3) Finally, we multiply each side of this last equation by 12.

$$12 \cdot \frac{y}{x} = 12 \cdot \frac{1}{6}$$
$$\frac{12y}{x} = 2$$

Questions 34 - 35 refer to the following information.

$$d = 456 - 3.02p$$

In the equation above d represents the demand (the quantity demanded), in units, of a certain product with a price of p dollars.

34. Which of the following expresses the price of the product in terms of the demand?

(A) $p = \dfrac{d+456}{3.02}$

(B) $p = \dfrac{d-456}{3.02}$

(C) $p = \dfrac{456-d}{3.02}$

(D) $p = \dfrac{3.02}{d+456}$

* Algebraic solution: To get p by itself we begin by subtracting 456 from each side of the equation to get $d - 456 = -3.02p$. We then divide each side of this last equation by -3.02 to get $p = \dfrac{d-456}{-3.02} = \dfrac{-(d-456)}{3.02} = \dfrac{456-d}{3.02}$. This is choice C.

Notes: (1) As an alternative, we can begin by adding $3.02p$ to each side of the given equation, and subtracting d from each side as well. This gives us $3.02p = 456 - d$. We then divide each side of this last equation by 3.02 to get $p = \dfrac{456-d}{3.02}$.

This alternative method has the advantage that a minus sign never appears in the denominator.

(2) $\dfrac{a}{-b} = \dfrac{-a}{b}$. So, in particular, $\dfrac{d-456}{-3.02} = \dfrac{-(d-456)}{3.02}$ (here $a = d - 456$ and $b = 3.02$.

(3) $-(x - y) = -x + y = y - x$. In particular, $-(d - 456) = 456 - d$ (here $x = d$ and $y = 456$).

(4) If a calculator is allowed, then this problem can also be solved by picking numbers. In this case it is easiest to choose a value for p, and then determine the corresponding value for d in the original equation. We would then substitute the d value into each answer choice and eliminate any choices for which p comes out incorrect. I leave the details of this solution to the reader.

35. * For which of the following prices will the demand be closest to 314 units.

   (A) $44
   (B) $45
   (C) $46
   (D) $47

Solution by starting with choice C: We start with choice C and guess that $p = 46$. It follows that $d = 456 - 3.02 \cdot 46 = 317.08$. This seems like it is probably a bit too large.

Let's try D next and let $p = 47$. Then $d = 456 - 3.02 \cdot 47 = 314.06$. Since this is closer, the answer is D.

* Solution by using the answer to the last problem: From the last problem we know that $p = \frac{456-d}{3.02}$. We substitute 314 in for d to get

$$p = \frac{456 - 314}{3.02} = \frac{142}{3.02} \approx 47.02$$

So the answer is choice D.

36. A pipe is used to fill a swimming pool with water. The amount of water in the pool is given by the equation $V = 12t + 200$, where t is the number of minutes since the pipe began filling the pool and V is the volume, in gallons, of water in the pool. In the equation, what are the meanings of the numbers 12 and 200 ?

   (A) The number 12 is the rate of increase, in gallons per minute, in the volume of the water in the pool, and the number 200 is the initial number of gallons of water in the pool.

   (B) The number 12 is the rate of decrease, in gallons per minute, in the volume of the water in the pool, and the number 200 is the initial number of gallons of water in the pool.

   (C) The number 12 is the rate of decrease, in gallons per minute, in the volume of the water in the pool, and the pool holds 200 gallons of water.

   (D) The number 12 is the number of minutes it will take to fill the pool, and the pool holds 200 gallons of water.

50

Solution by picking numbers: If $t = 0$, then $V = 200$. So the initial number of gallons of water in the pool is 200.

If $t = 1$, then $V = 12 \cdot 1 + 200 = 212$. So when the number of minutes increases by 1, the number of gallons of water increases by 12.

So the answer is choice A.

* Algebraic solution: The equation is linear with a slope of $12 = \frac{12}{1}$. This means that an increase in t by 1 unit corresponds to an increase in V by 12 units.

In a linear equation, the constant term is the value of the dependent variable when the independent variable is 0. In this case that means that the volume is 200 at time 0.

So the answer is choice A.

Notes: (1) In the equation $V = 12t + 200$, we are thinking of t as the **independent variable**, and V as the **dependent variable**. In other words, we input a value for t, and we get a V value as an output.

For example, if the input is $t = 1$ minutes, then the output is a volume of $V = 12 \cdot 1 + 200 = 212$ gallons of water.

(2) Recall that the slope of a line is

$$\text{Slope} = m = \frac{\text{change in the dependent variable}}{\text{change in the independent variable}} = \frac{\text{change in } V}{\text{change in } t}$$

(3) The **slope-intercept form of an equation of a line** is $y = mx + b$ where m is the slope of the line.

In the given equation, $V = 12t + 200$, the slope is $m = 12 = \frac{12}{1}$.

(4) Combining notes (2) and (3), we see that a change in t by 1 unit corresponds to a change in V by 12 units.

(5) Since the sign of 12 is positive ($12 = +12$), there is a **positive association** between t and V. It follows that an increase in t corresponds to an increase in V.

(6) As an example with a **negative association** between two variables, consider the equation

$$y = -12x + 200$$

In this equation the slope of the linear equation is $-12 = -\frac{12}{1}$. A change in x by 1 unit corresponds to a change in y by 12 units, but this time an increase in x corresponds to a *decrease* in y.

37. A file of size 2.7 gigabytes is being transferred at an average rate of 25.3 megabytes per minute. Which of the following functions can be used to estimate how many megabytes, $M(t)$, remain to be transferred after t minutes? (1 gigabyte is approximately equal to 1,000 megabytes.)

(A) $M(t) = 0.0253 - 2.7t$
(B) $M(t) = 2.7 - 0.0253t$
(C) $M(t) = 25.3 - 2,700t$
(D) $M(t) = 2,700 - 25.3t$

* **Algebraic solution:** 2.7 gigabytes is equal to $2.7 \cdot 1000 = 2,700$ megabytes. After t minutes, $25.3t$ megabytes have been transferred, and so $2700 - 25.3t$ megabytes remain to be transferred, choice D.

Notes: (1) 1 gigabyte is equivalent to 1,000 megabytes, it follows that 2.7 gigabytes is equivalent to $2.7 \cdot 1000 = 2,700$ megabytes.

(2) We can also convert between megabytes and gigabytes more formally by setting up a ratio.

	1,000	x
megabyte	1,000	x
gigabyte	1	2.7

We now find x by cross multiplying and dividing.

$$\frac{1000}{1} = \frac{x}{2.7}$$
$$1x = 2.7 \cdot 1000$$
$$x = 2,700$$

(3) After 1 minute, 25.3 megabytes have been transferred. After 2 minutes, $25.3 \cdot 2 = 50.6$ megabytes have been transferred. After 3 minutes, $25.3 \cdot 3 = 75.9$ megabytes have been transferred. And so on... In general, after t minutes, $25.3t$ megabytes have been transferred.

(4) To find the number of megabytes that have not been transferred, we subtract the amount that has been transferred ($25.3t$) from the initial amount (2,700) to get $2,700 - 25.3t$.

52

Solution using the initial amount: The initial amount that needs to be transferred is 2.7 gigabytes, which is equivalent to 2,700 megabytes. This means that if we substitute 0 for t, the result should be 2,700. Let's check each choice.

> (A) $M(0) = 0.0253$
> (B) $M(0) = 2.7$
> (C) $M(0) = 25.3$
> (D) $M(0) = 2,700$

Since choices A, B and C came out incorrect, the answer is choice D.

Notes: (1) This is an example of the strategy of "picking numbers." The number we chose to use here was $t = 0$.

(2) This strategy can be used only to eliminate answer choices. Make sure that you check every answer choice, even if one of the answers comes out correct. If more than one choice comes out correct, you must pick new numbers, and use them in the remaining choices.

(3) When picking numbers, I generally suggest avoiding numbers as simple as 0 or 1 (but 2 is usually a great choice). Sometimes, however, it is worth trying these simple numbers, if it won't take too much time to do so, and the computations might prove tedious with larger numbers. Just be aware that when using 0 or 1 it is likely that more than one choice will come out correct. In this case, we got lucky (and sometimes on the actual test you will get lucky too).

38. If $27 - 7x$ is 11 less than 17, what is the value of $3x$?

* Algebraic solution: 11 less than 17 is $17 - 11 = 6$. So we are given that $27 - 7x$ is 6. In other words, we should solve the equation $27 - 7x = 6$. We subtract 27 from each side to get $-7x = 6 - 27 = -21$. Finally, we divide each side of this last equation by -7 to get $x = \frac{-21}{-7} = $ **3**.

Note: A common mistake would be to interpret "11 less than 17" as $11 - 17$ which would give a result of -6. This is **wrong!**

"11 less than 17" should always be interpreted as $17 - 11$.

$$\sqrt{10b^2 - 9} + x = 0$$

39. If $b > 0$ and $x = -9$ in the equation above, what is the value of b ?

Solution by taking a guess: When we replace x by -9 we get

$$\sqrt{10b^2 - 9} - 9 = 0.$$

Let's start with a "random" guess for b, let's say $b = 5$. So let's plug 5 in for b in the equation above.

$$\sqrt{10(5)^2 - 9} - 9 = \sqrt{10 \cdot 25 - 9} - 9 = \sqrt{250 - 9} - 9 = \sqrt{241} - 9.$$

Since $\sqrt{241} > 9$, our guess was too big.

Let's try $b = 3$ next. We then have the following.

$$\sqrt{10(3)^2 - 9} - 9 = \sqrt{90 - 9} - 9 = \sqrt{81} - 9 = 9 - 9 = 0.$$

So the answer is **3**.

* Algebraic solution: As in the previous solution we replace x by -9 to get

$$\sqrt{10b^2 - 9} - 9 = 0, \text{ or equivalently, } \sqrt{10b^2 - 9} = 9$$

We square each side of this last equation to get $10b^2 - 9 = 81$.

We then add 9 to get $10b^2 = 90$, and then divide by 10 to get $b^2 = 9$. Since $3^2 = 9$, the answer is **3**.

Remark: To solve the equation $b^2 = 9$ formally requires the **square root property**. There are two solutions to this equation: $b = 3$ and $b = -3$. See problem 20 for more on the square root property.

40. * A factory owner has a maximum daily budget of $12,000. The factory makes n identical items, each costing $17 to produce. If the daily fixed costs to run the factory are $8,500, what is the maximum possible value for n that will keep the combined daily fixed costs and production costs within the factory owner's daily budget?

* Algebraic solution: We need to find the largest integer n for which

$$17n + 8500 < 12,000.$$

We subtract 8500 from each side of this inequality to get

$$17n < 12,000 - 8500$$
$$17n < 3500$$

We now divide each side of this last inequality by 17 to get

$$n < \frac{3500}{17} \approx 205.88$$

So we grid in **205**.

Notes: (1) The cost to produce 1 item is 17 dollars.

The cost to produce 2 items is $17 \cdot 2 = 34$ dollars.

The cost to produce 3 items is $17 \cdot 3 = 51$ dollars

In general, the cost to produce n items is $17n$ dollars.

(2) When we add the daily fixed costs to the cost to produce n items, we get $17n + 8500$ dollars.

(3) Once we get the answer 205, we can substitute this value back into the original inequality to make sure that it works:

$$17 \cdot 205 + 8500 = 11,985$$

Since $11,985 < 12,000$, producing 205 items keeps the costs within the factory owner's daily budget.

(4) To be extra safe, let's make sure that 206 fails:

$$17 \cdot 206 + 8500 = 12,002$$

Since $12,002 > 12,000$, 206 items is too many, and we see that the maximum possible acceptable number of items is 205.

(5) This problem can also be solved by taking guesses for n. I leave the details of this solution to the reader.

LEVEL 2: GEOMETRY AND TRIG

41. A line in the xy-plane passes through the origin and has a slope of $-\frac{2}{3}$. Which of the following points lies on the line?

 (A) $(-6, 4)$
 (B) $(3, -3)$
 (C) $(3, 2)$
 (D) $(0, \frac{2}{3})$

* Solution by writing an equation and plugging in the points: An equation of the line is $y = -\frac{2}{3}x$. Let's start with choice C and replace x by 3. We then get $y = -\frac{2}{3}(3) = -2$. So we can eliminate choices B and C.

Let's try A next and replace x by -6. We get $y = -\frac{2}{3}(-6) = 4$. This is correct, and so the answer is choice A.

Notes: (1) The origin is the point $(0, 0)$. If the origin is a point on the line, then it is the y-intercept of the line.

(2) The equation of a line in slope-intercept form is $y = mx + b$, where m is the slope of the line, and the point $(0, b)$ is the y-intercept of the line.

In this problem we are given that the point $(0, 0)$ is on the line, so that $b = 0$. We are also given that the slope is $m = -\frac{2}{3}$.

So the equation of the line in slope-intercept form is

$$y = -\frac{2}{3}x + 0, \text{ or equivalently } y = -\frac{2}{3}x.$$

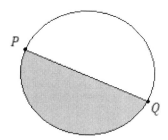

42. In the circle above, segment PQ is a diameter. If the area of the shaded region is 18π, what is the length of the diameter of the circle?

    (A) 6
    (B) 9
    (C) 12
    (D) 18

* A diameter divides a circle into two equal halves. It follows that the area of the circle is $2 \cdot 18\pi = 36\pi$. So the radius of the circle is 6, and therefore the diameter of the circle is 12, choice C.

Notes: (1) The area of a circle is $A = \pi r^2$. In this problem we found that the area is 36π. So we have $36\pi = \pi r^2$. Dividing each side of this equation by π gives us $36 = r^2$. So $r = \sqrt{36} = 6$.

(2) The equation $36 = r^2$ has two solutions $r = \pm 6$. Since a radius must be positive, we reject the negative solution.

(3) The diameter of a circle is twice the radius. Symbolically, $d = 2r$.

43. In the xy-plane, the point $(0, 3)$ is the center of a circle that has radius 3. Which of the following is NOT a point on the circle?

   (A) $(0, 6)$
   (B) $(-3, 6)$
   (C) $(3, 3)$
   (D) $(-3, 3)$

* Solution by drawing a picture:

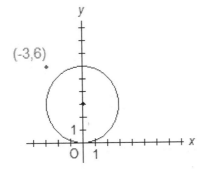

From the picture it should be clear that $(-3, 6)$ is not on the circle. This is choice B.

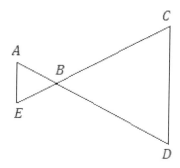

44. In the figure above, $\overline{AE} \parallel \overline{CD}$, $\overline{AB} \cong \overline{BE}$, and $m\angle ABE = 40°$. What is the measure, in degrees, of angle C ? (Disregard the degree sign when gridding in your answer.)

* $m\angle C = m\angle E = \dfrac{180-40}{2} = \dfrac{140}{2} = 70°$. So we grid in **70**.

Notes: (1) The symbol $\parallel$ stands for "parallel," so that $\overline{AE} \parallel \overline{CD}$ is read "segment AE is parallel to segment CD."

(2) The symbol $\cong$ stands for "congruent," so that $\overline{AB} \cong \overline{BE}$ is read "line segment AB is congruent to line segment BE."

Two line segments are **congruent** if they have the same length. Two angles are **congruent** if they have the same measure. Two triangles are **congruent** if all corresponding sides and interior angles are congruent.

(3) $m\angle ABE$ is read "the measure of angle ABE." So we are given "the measure of angle ABE is 40 degrees."

(4) In the given figure, line segments $\overline{AE}$ and $\overline{CD}$ are cut by the transversal $\overline{AD}$.

$\angle A$ and $\angle D$ are called **alternate interior angles.**

$\angle E$ and $\angle C$ are also alternate interior angles.

(5) Since the line segments $\overline{AE}$ and $\overline{CD}$ happen to be parallel, the alternate interior angles formed are congruent. This is known as the **alternate interior angle theorem.**

In particular, $\angle C \cong \angle E$ and so $m\angle C = m\angle E$.

(6) Since $\overline{AB} \cong \overline{BE}$, ΔABE is isosceles. It follows that $m\angle A = m\angle E$.

(7)Tthe sum of the measures of a triangle add to $180°$. So we have

58

$$m\angle A + m\angle ABE + m\angle E = 180°$$
$$m\angle E + 40° + m\angle E = 180°$$
$$2m\angle E = 180° - 40° = 140°$$
$$m\angle E = \frac{140}{2} = 70°$$

The following notes are useful, but not needed for the solution method that we used here.

(8) $\angle ABE$ and $\angle CBD$ are **vertical angles**. Vertical angles are congruent.

(9) $\triangle ABE \sim \triangle CBD$

The symbol $\sim$ stands for "similar," so that $\triangle ABE \sim \triangle CBD$ is read "triangle ABE is similar to triangle CBD."

Two triangles are **similar** if they have the same angle measures.

(10) To determine that two triangles are similar, it is sufficient to show that two pairs of angles have the same measure. We get the third pair for free because the angle measures in a triangle always sum to $180°$.

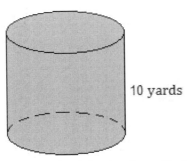

10 yards

45. A tank in the shape of a right circular cylinder is completely filled with water as shown above. If the volume of the tank is 160π cubic yards, what is the <u>diameter</u> of the base of the cylinder, in yards?

* Algebraic solution:

$$V = \pi r^2 h$$
$$160\pi = \pi r^2 (10)$$
$$16 = r^2$$
$$4 = r.$$

So $d = 2r = 2 \cdot 4 = \mathbf{8}$.

Notes: (1) The volume of a cylinder is $V = \pi r^2 h$ where r is the radius of a base of the cylinder, and h is the height of the cylinder.

(2) To get from the second to the third equation, we divided each side of the equation by 10π

(3) The equation $16 = r^2$ would normally have the two solutions $\pm 4 = r$. But the radius of a circle must be positive, and so we reject the negative solution.

(4) The diameter of a circle is twice the radius. Symbolically, $d = 2r$.

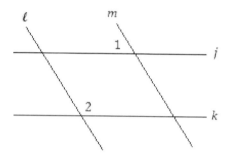

46. In the figure above, lines j and k are parallel and lines l and m are parallel. If the measure of $\angle 1$ is $57°$, what is the measure of $\angle 2$? (Disregard the degree sign when gridding in your answer.)

* $m\angle 2 = 180° - m\angle 1 = 180° - 57° = 123°$. So we grid in **123**.

Notes: (1) Whenever parallel lines are cut by a transversal, eight angles are formed. Any two of these angles are either congruent (they have the same measure) or supplementary (their measures sum to $180°$).

(2) $\angle 1$ and $\angle 2$ are clearly not congruent ($\angle 1$ is acute and $\angle 2$ is obtuse). So they must be supplementary. This means $m\angle 1 + m\angle 2 = 180°$.

(3) The following figure shows two parallel lines cut by the transversal ℓ.

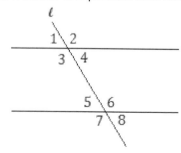

60

Angles 1, 4, 5, and 8 all have the same measure. Also, angles 2, 3, 6, and 7 all have the same measure. Any two angles that do not have the same measure are supplementary, that is their measures add to 180°.

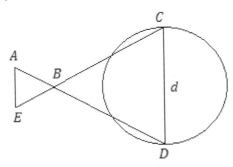

47. An ecologist wants to find the diameter, d, in meters, of a circular plot of land as represented in the sketch above. The lengths represented by AE, EB, BC, and BD on the sketch were determined to be 2300 meters, 2800 meters, 4200 meters, and 4000 meters, respectively. Segments AD and CE intersect at B, and $\angle EAB$ and $\angle CDB$ have the same measure. What is the value of d ?

* $\frac{CD}{AE} = \frac{BC}{EB}$. Thus, $\frac{d}{2300} = \frac{4200}{2800} = \frac{3}{2}$. So $d = \frac{3}{2} \cdot 2300 = \textbf{3450}$.

Notes: (1) The two triangles are similar. See problem 44 for more information about similar triangles.

(2) **Corresponding sides of similar triangles are in proportion**. So for example, in the figure above $\frac{CD}{AE} = \frac{BC}{EB}$.

(3) BD was not needed to answer the question.

48. If $0 \leq x \leq 90°$ and $\sin x = \frac{12}{13}$, then $\tan x =$

* **Trigonometric solution:** Let's draw a picture. We begin with a right triangle and label one of the angles x.

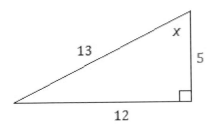

Since $\sin x = \dfrac{\text{OPP}}{\text{HYP}}$, we label the leg opposite x with a 12 and the hypotenuse with 13. We can use the Pythagorean triple 5, 12, 13 to see that the other side is 5.

Finally, $\tan x = \dfrac{\text{OPP}}{\text{ADJ}} = $ **12/5** or **2. 4**.

Notes: (1) The most common Pythagorean triples are 3, 4, 5 and 5, 12, 13. Two others that may come up are 8, 15, 17 and 7, 24, 25.

(2) If you don't remember the Pythagorean triple 5, 12, 13, you can use the Pythagorean Theorem (see problem 10):

Here we have $a^2 + 12^2 = 13^2$. Therefore $a^2 + 144 = 169$. Subtracting 144 from each side of this equation gives $a^2 = 169 - 144 = 25$. Therefore, $a = 5$.

(3) The equation $a^2 = 25$ would normally have two solutions: $a = 5$ and $a = -5$. But the length of a side of a triangle cannot be negative, so we reject -5.

LEVEL 2: PASSPORT TO ADVANCED MATH

$$h(x) = |x^2 - 5| + 1$$

49. For what value of x is $h(x)$ equal to 0?

(A) 0
(B) 1
(C) $\sqrt{5}$
(D) There is no such value of x

Solution by starting with choice C: We start with choice C and compute $h(\sqrt{5}) = |(\sqrt{5})^2 - 5| + 1 = |5 - 5| + 1 = 0 + 1 = 1$.

So we can eliminate choice C.

Let's try B: $h(1) = |1^2 - 5| + 1 = |1 - 5| + 1 = |-4| + 1 = 4 + 1 = 5$.

So we can eliminate choice B.

Let's try A: $h(0) = |-5| + 1 = 5 + 1 = 6$.

So we can eliminate choice A and the answer is choice D.

* **Direct solution:** $|x^2 - 5| \geq 0$ no matter what x is. It follows that $|x^2 - 5| + 1 \geq 1$.

In particular, $|x^2 - 5| + 1$ could never be 0, and so the answer is D.

Recall: $|x|$ is the **absolute value** of x. If x is nonnegative, then $|x| = x$. If x is negative, then $|x| = -x$ (in other words, if x is negative, then taking the absolute value just eliminates the minus sign). For example, $|12| = 12$ and $|-12| = 12$.

$$g(x) = (x + 3)^2 - 16$$

50. Which of the following is a value of x that satisfies $g(x) = 0$?

    (A) -8
    (B) -7
    (C)   0
    (D)   7

* **Solution by starting with choice C:** Let's start with choice C and compute $g(0) = (0 + 3)^2 - 16 = 3^2 - 16 = 9 - 16 = -7$. Since $g(0) \neq 0$, we can eliminate choice C.

Let's try B: $g(-7) = (-7 + 3)^2 - 16 = (-4)^2 - 16 = 16 - 16 = 0$. So $g(-7) = 0$, and the answer is choice B.

Note: $(-4)^2 = (-4)(-4) = 16$.

Algebraic solution: We solve the equation $g(x) = 0$.

$$(x + 3)^2 - 16 = 0$$
$$(x + 3)^2 = 16$$
$$x + 3 = \pm 4$$

$$x + 3 = -4 \quad \text{or} \quad x + 3 = 4$$
$$x = -4 - 3 = -7 \quad \text{or} \quad x = 4 - 3 = 1$$

So $x = -7$ or $x = 1$. Since -7 is an answer choice, the answer is B.

Notes: (1) The equation $(x + 3)^2 = 16$ has two solutions: $x + 3 = 4$ and $x + 3 = -4$. A common mistake is to forget about the negative solution.

(2) The **square root property** says that if $x^2 = c$, then $x = \pm\sqrt{c}$.

This is different from taking the positive square root of a number. For example, $\sqrt{4} = 2$, whereas the equation $x^2 = 4$ has two solutions $x = \pm 2$.

$$(x^3 - 3x^2y + 2xy^2 - y^3) - (-x^3 - 3x^2y - 2xy^2 - y^3)$$

51. Which of the following is equivalent to the expression above?

(A) 0
(B) $x^3 + y^3$
(C) $-6x^2y - 2y^3$
(D) $2x^3 + 4xy^2$

* Algebraic solution:

$$(x^3 - 3x^2y + 2xy^2 - y^3) - (-x^3 - 3x^2y - 2xy^2 - y^3)$$
$$= x^3 - 3x^2y + 2xy^2 - y^3 + x^3 + 3x^2y + 2xy^2 + y^3$$
$$= (x^3 + x^3) + (-3x^2y + 3x^2y) + (2xy^2 + 2xy^2) + (-y^3 + y^3)$$
$$= 2x^3 + 0 + 4xy^2 + 0 = 2x^3 + 4xy^2, \text{ choice D.}$$

Solution by picking numbers: Let's let $x = y = 1$. Then

$$(x^3 - 3x^2y + 2xy^2 - y^3) - (-x^3 - 3x^2y - 2xy^2 - y^3)$$
$$= (1 - 3 + 2 - 1) - (-1 - 3 - 2 - 1)$$
$$= -1 - (-7)$$
$$= -1 + 7$$
$$= 6$$

Put a nice big dark circle around 6 so you can find it easier later. We now substitute $x = y = 1$ into each answer choice:

(A) 0
(B) $1 + 1 = 2$
(C) $-6 - 2 = -8$
(D) $2 + 4 = 6$

Since A, B and C each came out incorrect, the answer is choice D.

Notes: (1) D is **not** the correct answer simply because it is equal to 6. It is correct because all three of the other choices are **not 6. You absolutely must check all four choices!**

(2) See problem 1 for more information on picking numbers.

(3) Substituting 1 in for all of the variables in a polynomial is equivalent to adding up all the coefficients of the polynomial.

For example, when we plug in 1 for x and y into the expression

$$x^3 - 3x^2y + 2xy^2 - y^3$$

we get $1 - 3 + 2 - 1 = -1$.

52. What are the solutions to the equation $5x^2 - 245 = 0$?

   (A) $-\sqrt{245}$ and $\sqrt{245}$
   (B) $-\frac{\sqrt{245}}{5}$ and $\frac{\sqrt{245}}{5}$
   (C) -49 and 49
   (D) -7 and 7

Solution by starting with choice C: Let's start with choice C and try the positive value 49. A moment's thought should make you realize that 49^2 is too large already.

Let's check choice D: $5(7)^2 = 5 \cdot 49 = 245$. So we do in fact have that $5x^2 - 245 = 5(7)^2 - 245 = 245 - 245 = 0$.

So the answer is choice D.

Notes: (1) If we are allowed to use a calculator for this problem, then we can simply plug the numbers into our calculator. For example, to check $x = 7$ we would type $5 * 7\text{^}2 - 245$, and the output will give 0.

(2) Squaring a negative number gives the same result as squaring the corresponding positive number, and so in this problem we need check only the positive values.

For example, 7^2 and $(-7)^2$ are both equal to 49

* Algebraic solution: We start by dividing each side of the given equation by 5 to get $x^2 - 49 = 0$. Adding 49 gives us $x^2 = 49$. Finally, we use the square root property to get $x = \pm 7$, choice D.

Notes: (1) The equation $x^2 = 49$ has two solutions: $x = 7$ and $x = -7$. A common mistake is to forget about the negative solution.

(2) To solve the equation $x^2 = 49$ formally requires the **square root property**. There are two solutions to this equation: $x = 7$ and $x = -7$. See problem 20 for more on the square root property.

(3) Another way to solve the equation $x^2 - 49 = 0$ is to factor the difference of two squares as follows:

$$x^2 - 49 = 0$$
$$(x - 7)(x + 7) = 0$$

We now set each factor equal to 0 to get $x - 7 = 0$ or $x + 7 = 0$.

So $x = 7$ or $x = -7$.

(4) We can also solve the equation $5x^2 - 245 = 0$ by first adding 245 to each side of the equation to get $5x^2 = 245$. We then divide by 5 to get $x^2 = \frac{245}{5} = 49$. Finally, we apply the square root property to get $x = \pm 7$.

$$2(x - 3)(2x + 1)$$

53.   Which of the following is equivalent to the expression above?

    (A) $-12x$
    (B) $4x^2 - 6$
    (C) $6x^2 - 4$
    (D) $4x^2 - 10x - 6$

Solution by picking a number: Let's let $x = 4$. Then we have

$$2(x - 3)(2x + 1) = 2(4 - 3)(2 \cdot 4 + 1) = 2 \cdot 1 \cdot 9 = \textbf{18}.$$

Put a nice big dark circle around 18 so you can find it easier later. We now substitute $x = 4$ into each answer choice:

    (A) $-12 \cdot 4 = -36$
    (B) $4 \cdot 4^2 - 6 = 4 \cdot 16 - 6 = 64 - 6 = 58$
    (C) $6 \cdot 4^2 - 4 = 6 \cdot 16 - 4 = 96 - 4 = 92$
    (D) $4 \cdot 4^2 - 10 \cdot 4 - 6 = 4 \cdot 16 - 40 - 6 = 64 - 46 = 18$

Since A, B, and C each came out incorrect, the answer is choice **D.**

Important note: D is **not** the correct answer simply because it is equal to 18. It is correct because all three of the other choices are **not 18. You absolutely must check all four choices!**

* Algebraic solution:

$$2(x - 3)(2x + 1) = 2(2x^2 + x - 6x - 3) = 2(2x^2 - 5x - 3)$$
$$= 4x^2 - 10x - 6$$

Notes: (1) In the solution above we multiplied the polynomials $(x - 3)$ and $(2x + 1)$ by FOILing.

66

(2) Here is an alternative method for multiplying the two polynomials.

We begin by lining up the polynomials vertically:

$$x - 3$$
$$2x + 1$$

We multiply the 1 on the bottom by each term on top, moving from right to left. First note that 1 times -3 is -3:

$$x - 3$$
$$\underline{2x + 1}$$
$$- 3$$

Next note that 1 times x is x:

$$x - 3$$
$$\underline{2x + 1}$$
$$x - 3$$

Now we multiply the $2x$ on the bottom by each term on top, moving from right to left. This time as we write the answers we leave one blank space on the right:

$$x - 3$$
$$\underline{2x + 1}$$
$$x - 3$$
$$\underline{2x^2 - 6x}$$

Finally, we add:

$$x - 3$$
$$\underline{2x + 1}$$
$$x - 3$$
$$\underline{2x^2 - 6x}$$
$$2x^2 - 5x - 3$$

$$5(-4x^3 - x + 1) - 2(x^3 - 2x^2 - 5x) = ax^3 + bx^2 + cx + d$$

54. In the equation above, a, b, c, and d are constants. If the equation is true for all values of x, what is the value of c ?

* Quick solution: Since c is the coefficient of x, we simply compute

$$5(-x) - 2(-5x) = -5x + 10x = 5x.$$

It follows that $c = \textbf{5}$.

Complete computation:

$$5(-4x^3 - x + 1) - 2(x^3 - 2x^2 - 5x)$$

$$= -20x^3 - 5x + 5 - 2x^3 + 4x^2 + 10x$$

$$= -22x^3 + 4x^2 + 5x + 5$$

So we have $-22x^3 + 4x^2 + 5x + 5 = ax^3 + bx^2 + cx + d$.

It follows that $a = -22$, $b = 4$, $c = 5$, and $d = 5$.

In particular, $c = \mathbf{5}$.

$$x^4(x^2 - 10) = -9x^2$$

55. What is one possible positive solution to the equation above?

* Solution by guessing: Since this is a Level 2 problem, a simple guess should work. Let's try $x = 1$. Then we have

$$1^4(1^2 - 10) = -9 \cdot 1^2$$
$$1(1 - 10) = -9 \cdot 1$$
$$1(-9) = -9$$
$$-9 = -9$$

Since this last equation is true, a solution is **1**.

Algebraic solution:

$$x^4(x^2 - 10) = -9x^2$$
$$x^6 - 10x^4 = -9x^2$$
$$x^6 - 10x^4 + 9x^2 = 0$$
$$x^2(x^4 - 10x^2 + 9) = 0$$
$$x^2(x^2 - 1)(x^2 - 9) = 0$$
$$x^2(x - 1)(x + 1)(x - 3)(x + 3) = 0$$

We see that the solutions to this equation are $x = \pm 1$ and $x = \pm 3$.

Since we want a positive solution, we can grid in either **1** or **3**.

Notes: (1) Some students might find it hard to see how to factor the expression $x^4 - 10x^2 + 9$.

To help see how to do this we can make a formal substitution of $u = x^2$. The expression then becomes $u^2 - 10u + 9$. This expression factors as $(u - 1)(u - 9)$. We can then replace u by x^2 to get $(x^2 - 1)(x^2 - 9)$.

(2) The expression $x^2 - a^2$ factors as $(x - a)(x + a)$.

If $a = 1$, we get $x^2 - 1 = (x - 1)(x + 1)$.

If $a = 3$, we get $x^2 - 9 = (x - 3)(x + 3)$.

56. A function f satisfies $f(5) = 2$ and $f(7) = 1$. A function g satisfies $g(8) = 5$ and $g(1) = 4$. Find the value of $f(g(8))$.

* $f(g(8)) = f(5) = 2$.

Note: $g(8)$ is given to be 5. So we replace $g(8)$ by 5 in the expression $f(g(8))$.

Do you see that we have $f(\boxed{\text{something}})$ where $\boxed{\text{something}}$ is $g(8)$? Since $g(8)$ is 5, we can replace $\boxed{\text{something}}$ by 5 to get $f(5)$. Finally, $f(5)$ is given to be 2.

LEVEL 2: PROBLEM SOLVING AND DATA

Questions 57 - 58 refer to the following information.

	Salary Range				
	Less than $60,000	$60,000-$89,999	$90,000-$120,000	Greater than $120,000	Total
Male	15	76	18	23	134
Female	9	21	86	9	123
Total	24	97	104	32	257

57. * A group of engineers responded to a survey that asked what their annual salary was. The survey data were broken down as shown in the table above. Which of the following categories accounts for approximately 7 percent of all the survey respondents?

(A) Males making less than $60,000
(B) Males making between $90,000 and $120,000
(C) Males making greater than $120,000
(D) Females making between $60,000 and $89,999

* **Solution by starting with choice C:** Note that a total of 257 engineers were surveyed.

Let's start with choice C and observe that there are 23 males making greater than $120,000. So we get a percentage of $\frac{23}{257} \approx 0.08949 \approx 9\%$.

Let's try choice B next and observe that there are 18 males making between $90,000 and $120,000. So this time we get a percentage of $\frac{18}{257} \approx .07 = 7\%$. Therefore, the answer is B.

Note: In this case, starting with choice C is actually not really the most efficient first choice. The reason for this is that 23 is the largest of the numbers we will be looking at in the table.

The numbers in the table that we are concerned with are 15, 18, 23, and 21. So to be more efficient we may have wanted to start with 18 (choice B) or 21 (choice D).

58. * If an engineer is selected at random, what is the probability that this engineer will be a female making between $90,000 and $120,000 to the nearest tenth?

    (A) 0.3
    (B) 0.4
    (C) 0.6
    (D) 0.8

* The total number of engineers is 257, and the number of these engineers that are females making between $90,000 and $120,000 is 86. So the desired probability is $\frac{86}{257} \approx 0.33463$. To the nearest tenth, this is 0.3, choice A.

Note: To compute a simple probability where all outcomes are equally likely, we divide the number of "successes" by the total number of outcomes.

In this problem, a "success" would be selecting a female making between $90,000 and $120,000. The number of successes can be found by looking in the row labeled "Female" and the column labeled "$90,000-$120,000." So the number of successes is 86.

The "total" is the number of engineers surveyed. This number can be found in the lower right hand corner of the table. So the total is 257.

Weight of Cat (in pounds)

2	8	8	8	9	9	9
9	9	9	10	10	10	10
10	11	12	12	12	12	12
13	13	14	15	17	17	17
17	18	18	19	19	19	20

59. The table above lists the weights, to the nearest pound, of a random sample of 35 domestic shorthair cats. The outlier weight of 2 pounds is an error. Of the mean, median, mode, and range of the values listed, which will change the most if the 2-pound outlier is removed from the data?

   (A) Mean
   (B) Median
   (C) Mode
   (D) Range

* The median and mode do not change at all if we remove the 2, and the mean will change just a bit. The range however changes from 18 to 12 (a change of 6). So the answer is D.

Notes: (1) We can find the median (of the original set of data) quite easily by crossing out the top two and bottom two rows, and then just looking at the center of the middle row.

2	8	8	8	9	9	9
9	9	9	10	10	10	10
10	11	12	12	12	12	12
13	13	14	15	17	17	17
17	18	18	19	19	19	20

Now note that if we remove the 2 from the data, then the median will still be 12.

(2) The mode of the data is 9 because 9 appears 6 times, and no other number appears that many times. Deleting the 2 does not affect this, and so the mode remains 9.

71

(3) The range of the original data is $20 - 2 = 18$. When we remove the 2, the range becomes $20 - 8 = 12$.

(4) Computing the exact mean here would be quite tedious. But there is no need to do so. We need only be convinced that the mean will not change by 6 ($18 - 12 = 6$) when we remove the 2.

This should be somewhat obvious, but in case it is not, let's analyze this a bit. To compute the mean, we add up all the data, and then divide by the number of data points.

So to get the mean of all the data, we add everything up and divide by 35. For example, if all those numbers added up to 200, we would get a mean of $\frac{200}{35} \approx 5.7$.

To get the mean of the data with the 2 removed, we add everything except the 2, and divide by 34. So using our rough estimate for a sum of 200 for all the data, when we remove the 2 we get a sum of 198, and so we get a new mean of $\frac{198}{34} \approx 5.8$.

The change in the mean was approximately 0.1, a change that is much smaller than the change in range.

(5) It should be clear that even if our estimate was way off, the mean could not possibly have changed more than the range.

Definitions: The **average (arithmetic mean)** of a list of numbers is the sum of the numbers in the list divided by the quantity of the numbers in the list.

$$\textbf{Average } = \frac{\textbf{Sum}}{\textbf{Number}}$$

The **median** of a list of numbers is the middle number when the numbers are arranged in increasing order. If the total number of values in the list is even, then the median is the average of the two middle values.

The **mode** of a list of numbers is the number that occurs most frequently. There can be more than one mode if more than one number occurs with the greatest frequency.

The **range** of a list of numbers is the positive difference between the greatest number and smallest number in the list.

60. * The male spiny rock lobster has a maximum carapace length of 23.5 centimeters. Approximately what is the maximum carapace length of a male spiny rock lobster in <u>inches</u>? (1 inch ≈ 2.54 centimeters)

   (A) 0.11
   (B) 9.25
   (C) 18.5
   (D) 59.69

Solution by setting up a ratio: We identify 2 key words. Let's choose "centimeters" and "inches."

$$\begin{array}{ccc} \text{centimeters} & 23.5 & 2.54 \\ \text{inches} & x & 1 \end{array}$$

We now find x by cross multiplying and dividing.

$$\frac{23.5}{x} = \frac{2.54}{1}$$
$$2.54x = 23.5$$
$$x = \frac{23.5}{2.54} \approx 9.25$$

So the answer is choice B.

* Solution by estimating: 2.54 is approximately 2.5 and 23.5 is approximately 25. Since 2.5 goes into 25 ten times, we look for the answer closest to 10. This is choice B.

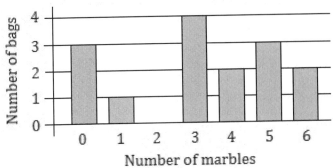

Number of Marbles in Each of 15 Bags

61. * Based on the histogram above, what is the average (arithmetic mean) number of marbles per bag?

73

$$* \frac{3 \cdot 0 + 1 \cdot 1 + 0 \cdot 2 + 4 \cdot 3 + 2 \cdot 4 + 3 \cdot 5 + 2 \cdot 6}{3 + 1 + 4 + 2 + 3 + 2} = \frac{1 + 12 + 8 + 15 + 12}{15} = \frac{48}{15} = \textbf{3.2}.$$

Notes: (1) According to the graph, 0 occurs 3 times, 1 occurs 1 time, 2 occurs 0 times, 3 occurs 4 times, 4 occurs 2 times, 5 occurs 3 times, and 6 occurs 2 times.

(2) A complete list of the data is

$$0, 0, 0, 1, 3, 3, 3, 3, 4, 4, 5, 5, 5, 6, 6$$

(3) Average $= \frac{\text{Sum}}{\text{Number}}$. In other words, to compute an average, we add up all the data, and then divide by the number of data points.

Questions 62 - 63 refer to the following information.

The amount of revenue that an online magazine retailer makes in a month is directly proportional to the number of active subscribers to the magazine. In July, the magazine had a total of 1200 subscribers, and the retailer reported revenue of $7200.

62. * In August, the online magazine had a total of 1500 subscribers. How much revenue did the retailer make? (Disregard the dollar sign when gridding in your answer).

Solution 1: Since the revenue, R, is directly proportional to the number of subscribers, x, $R = kx$ for some constant k. We are given that $R = 7200$ when $x = 1200$, so that $7200 = k(1200)$, or $k = \frac{7200}{1200} = 6$. Thus, $y = 6x$. When $x = 1500$, we have $y = 6 \cdot 1500 = \textbf{9000}$.

* Solution 2: Since R is directly proportional to x, $\frac{R}{x}$ is a constant. So we get the following ratio: $\frac{7200}{1200} = \frac{R}{1500}$. Cross multiplying gives $1200R = 7200 \cdot 1500$, or equivalently, $R = \frac{7200 \cdot 1500}{1200} = \textbf{9000}$.

Solution 3: The graph of $R = f(x)$ is a line passing through the points $(0, 0)$ and $(1200, 7200)$. The slope of this line is $\frac{7200 - 0}{1200 - 0} = 6$. Writing the equation of the line in slope-intercept form we have $y = 6x$. As in solution 1, when $x = 1500$, we have $y = 6 \cdot 1500 = \textbf{9000}$.

63. * The retailer uses 28% of the revenue each month for advertising. The rest of the money earned is the retailer's profit. What is the profit in a month where the magazine has 1200 subscribers?

* Quick solution: $0.72 \cdot 7200 = \mathbf{5184}$.

Notes: (1) If the magazine has 1200 subscribers, then the revenue for that month is 7200, as stated in the introductory paragraph.

(2) 28% of the revenue is $0.28 \cdot 7200 = 2016$ dollars. This is the amount that the retailer uses for advertising that month.

(3) The profit is equal to the revenue minus the advertising expense. For this month, that is $7200 - 2016 = 5184$ dollars.

(4) Taking 28% off of some amount is the same as taking $100 - 28 = 72\%$ of the same amount. So we can get the answer with a single computation as was done in the solution above.

$$A = 38t + 26$$

64. After making an initial deposit into a savings account, Theo proceeded to deposit a fixed amount of money into the same savings account each month. The equation above models the amount A, in dollars, that Theo has deposited after t monthly deposits. According to the model, how many dollars was Theo's initial deposit? (Disregard the $ sign when gridding your answer.)

* Quick solution: The initial deposit is the constant in the equation. So the answer is **26**.

Notes: (1) More formally, we get the initial deposit by substituting 0 for t into the equation: $A = 38 \cdot 0 + 26 = 0 + 26 = 26$.

(2) The equation $A = 38t + 26$ is linear. The independent variable is t and the dependent variable is A.

The graph of this equation is a line with slope 38 and y-intercept $(0, 26)$.

(3) 26 is the amount of the initial deposit and 38 is the amount of each of the other deposits after the initial one.

For example, after 1 month, we have $A = 38 \cdot 1 + 26 = 64$, so that there is 64 dollars in the account. Since there was previously 26 dollars in the account, the amount deposited after 1 month was $64 - 26 = 38$ dollars. (This note is not needed in this problem, but it could be useful for similar problems.)

LEVEL 3: HEART OF ALGEBRA

65. If $12x = 41$, what is the value of $4(x + \frac{1}{3})$?

(A) 15

(B) 14

(C) $\dfrac{83}{3}$

(D) $\dfrac{85}{12}$

Algebraic solution: We divide each side of the given equation by 12 to get $x = \frac{41}{12}$. It follows that $4\left(x + \frac{1}{3}\right) = 4\left(\frac{41}{12} + \frac{1}{3}\right) = 15$, choice A.

Notes: (1) If a calculator is allowed for this problem we can simply type the following in our calculator to get the answer:

$$4(41/ 12 + 1 / 3) \text{ ENTER}$$

(2) If a calculator is not allowed, then we would begin by rewriting $\frac{1}{3}$ as $\frac{1}{3} \cdot \frac{4}{4} = \frac{4}{12}$. We then have $\frac{41}{12} + \frac{1}{3} = \frac{41}{12} + \frac{4}{12} = \frac{41+4}{12} = \frac{45}{12}$. It then follows that $4\left(\frac{41}{12} + \frac{1}{3}\right) = 4\left(\frac{45}{12}\right) = \left(\frac{4}{12}\right)(45) = \left(\frac{1}{3}\right)(45) = 15$.

* Quicker algebraic solution: We divide each side of the given equation by 3 to get $4x = \frac{41}{3}$. We then have

$$4\left(x + \frac{1}{3}\right) = 4x + \frac{4}{3} = \frac{41}{3} + \frac{4}{3} = \frac{41 + 4}{3} = \frac{45}{3} = 15.$$

This is choice A.

$$w = 0.5a + 4.8$$

66. A paleontologist uses the model above to estimate the weight w of a certain species of dinosaur, in tons, in terms of the dinosaur's age a, in years. Based on the model, what is the estimated increase, in <u>pounds</u>, of the dinosaur's weight each year? (Note that 1 ton = 2000 pounds.)

    (A) 500
    (B) 1000
    (C) 1200
    (D) 2400

Solution by picking numbers: If $a = 1$, then $w = 0.5 + 4.8 = 5.3$. If $a = 2$, then $w = 0.5 \cdot 2 + 4.8 = 1 + 4.8 = 5.8$. So when the dinosaur's age increases by 1, the estimated weight of the dinosaur increases by $5.8 - 5.3 = 0.5$ tons. This is equivalent to $0.5 \cdot 2000 = 1000$ pounds, choice B.

* Algebraic solution: The equation is linear with a slope of $0.5 = \frac{0.5}{1}$. This means that an increase in a by 1 year corresponds to an increase in w by 0.5 tons. This is equivalent to 1000 pounds, choice B.

Notes: (1) In the equation $w = 0.5a + 4.8$, we are thinking of a as the **independent variable**, and w as the **dependent variable**. In other words, we input a value for a, and we get a w value as an output.

For example, if the input is $a = 2$ years, then the output is a weight of $w = 0.5 \cdot 2 + 4.8 = 1 + 4.8 = 5.8$ tons.

(2) Recall that the slope of a line is

$$\text{Slope} = m = \frac{\text{change in the dependent variable}}{\text{change in the independent variable}} = \frac{\text{change in } w}{\text{change in } a}$$

(3) The **slope-intercept form of an equation of a line** is $y = mx + b$ where m is the slope of the line.

The given equation is in slope-intercept form.

(4) Combining notes (2) and (3), we see that a change in a by 1 year corresponds to a change in w by 0.5 tons.

(5) Since the sign of 0.5 is positive ($0.5 = +0.5$), there is a **positive association** between a and w. It follows that an increase in a corresponds to an increase in w.

(6) As an example with a **negative association** between two variables, consider the equation

$$y = -3x + 25$$

In this equation the slope of the linear equation is $-3 = -\frac{3}{1}$. A change in x by 1 unit corresponds to a change in y by 3 units, but this time an increase in x corresponds to a *decrease* in y.

$$y = 2x + 9$$
$$x + 2y = 12$$

67. The system of equations above consists of two equations, and the graph of each equation in the xy-plane is a line. Which of the following statements is true about these two lines?

(A) The lines are the same.
(B) The lines are parallel, but distinct.
(C) The lines are perpendicular.
(D) The lines have the same y-intercept.

* Solution using slope-intercept form: The first equation is already in slope intercept form, and we see that the slope of the line is 2.

To get the second equation into slope-intercept form, we solve for y:

$$x + 2y = 12$$
$$2y = -x + 12$$
$$y = -\frac{1}{2}x + 6$$

We see that the slope of this second line is $-\frac{1}{2}$, and so the lines are perpendicular, choice C.

Notes: (1) The **slope-intercept form of an equation of a line** is

$$y = mx + b$$

where m is the slope of the line and b is the y-coordinate of the y-intercept, i.e. the point $(0, b)$ is on the line.

Note that the first equation is already in slope-intercept form, and its slope is $m = 2$

We put the second equation into slope-intercept form by solving for y, and we see that the slope of the second line is $-\frac{1}{2}$.

(2) Parallel lines have the same slope, and perpendicular lines have slopes that are negative reciprocals of each other.

(3) To solve the equation $2y = -x + 12$, we multiply each side of the equation by $\frac{1}{2}$ to get $y = \frac{1}{2}(-x + 12) = -\frac{1}{2}x + \frac{1}{2}(12) = -\frac{1}{2}x + 6$.

(4) The slope of the line with equation in the general form $ax + by = c$ is $m = -\frac{a}{b}$. In this question, for the second equation, we have $a = 1$ and $b = 2$. So the slope is $m = -\frac{1}{2}$.

Memorizing this little fact about the slope of a line in general form is optional. If you do know it, then it's a nice quick way to get the slope of a line in general form without having to do any algebra first. If you do not know it, then the first method of solution above is certainly acceptable.

(5) We can put the equation of a line in general form into slope-intercept form as follows:

$$ax + by = c$$
$$by = -ax + c$$
$$y = -\frac{a}{b}x + \frac{c}{b}$$

From this last equation we see that the slope is $m = -\frac{a}{b}$.

We were assuming that $b \neq 0$ of course.

68. The number of stuffed animals, q, that a toy company can sell per week at a price of p dollars is given by $q = 500 - 23p$. What is the meaning of the value 500 in this equation?

   (A) 500 dollars is the maximum that someone would pay for a stuffed animal.
   (B) 500 people per week would take a stuffed animal for free.
   (C) If the price of a stuffed animal is decreased by 1 dollar, then 500 more people will make a purchase.
   (D) If the price of a stuffed animal is decreased by 100 dollars, then 500 more people will make a purchase.

* $q = 500$ when $p = 0$. This means that the toy company can sell 500 stuffed animals per week at a price of 0 dollars. In other words, 500 people per week would take a stuffed animal for free, choice B.

Notes: (1) In the equation $q = 500 - 23p$, we are thinking of p as the **independent variable**, and q as the **dependent variable**. In other words, we input a value for p, and we get a q value as an output.

For example, if the input is a price of $p = 0$ dollars, then the output is a quantity of $q = 500 - 23(0) = 500$ stuffed animals.

(2) What if the question instead asked for the meaning of the number 23 in the equation?

First recall that the slope of a line is

$$\text{Slope} = m = \frac{\text{change in the dependent variable}}{\text{change in the independent variable}} = \frac{\text{change in } q}{\text{change in } p}$$

The **slope-intercept form of an equation of a line** is $y = mx + b$ where m is the slope of the line.

The given equation can be written $q = -23p + 500$, and we see that the slope is $m = -23 = -\frac{23}{1}$.

So we see that a change in p by 1 unit corresponds to a change in q by 23 units.

Since the sign of -23 is negative, there is a **negative association** between p and q. It follows that an increase in p corresponds to a decrease in q.

So if the price p of a stuffed animal is increased by 1 dollar, then 23 less people will make a purchase per week.

69. * Spencer took his cat Frisky to the vet for a checkup. The bill came to a total of $418. The expenses included a physical, a blood test, and a urinalysis. The cost of the blood test was 20 percent more than the cost of the physical and urinalysis combined. What did Spencer spend on Frisky's blood test?

 (A) 167
 (B) 190
 (C) 228
 (D) 348

80

* Algebraic solution: If we let x be the cost of the physical and urinalysis combined, then the cost of the blood test was $1.2x$. It follows that the total cost was $x + 1.2x = 2.2x$. Since we are given that the bill came to $418, we have $2.2x = 418$. It follows that $x = \frac{418}{2.2} = 190$.

So Spencer spent $1.2x = 1.2 \cdot 190 = 228$ dollars on Frisky's blood test, choice C.

Notes: (1) To compute 20 percent more than x we take 20% of x, and then add the result to x to get

$$x + 0.20x = (1 + 0.20)x = 1.20x = 1.2x.$$

Observe that $x = 1x$, and that the distributive property was used to factor out the x.

(2) We also used the distributive property to get

$$x + 1.2x = 1x + 1.2x = (1 + 1.2)x = 2.2x$$

(3) Be careful not to select 190 (choice B) as the answer. Once you find the value of x, you should always look back at the question to see if that is what they are asking for. In this problem we let x be the cost of the physical and urinalysis combined. But the question is asking for the cost of the blood test. This is $1.2x$.

70. A Japanese restaurant sells sushi for $4.50 per piece and sashimi for $3.00 per piece. The restaurant's revenue from selling a total of 216 pieces of sushi and sashimi in four hours was $781.50. How many pieces of sushi were sold during that four-hour period?

* Solution using the elimination method: Let's let x be the number of pieces of sushi sold, and y the number of pieces of sashimi sold. Then we are given the following system of equations.

$$x + y = 216$$
$$4.5x + 3y = 781.5$$

We will now multiply each side of the first equation by -3.

$$-3(x + y) = (216)(-3)$$
$$4.5x + 3y = 781.5$$

Do not forget to distribute correctly on the left. Add the two equations.

81

$$-3x - 3y = -648$$
$$\underline{4.5x + 3y = 781.5}$$
$$1.5x = 133.5$$

We divide each side of this last equation by 1.5 to get

$$x = \frac{133.5}{1.5} = \frac{1335}{15} = \mathbf{89}.$$

Notes: (1) We chose to multiply the first equation by -3 because multiplying by this number makes the y column "match up" so that when we add the two equations in the next step the y term vanishes.

(2) If we wanted to find y instead of x we would multiply the first equation by -4.5. In general, if you are looking for only one variable, try to eliminate the one you are **not** looking for.

(3) We chose to multiply by a negative number so that we could add the equations instead of subtracting them. We could have also multiplied the first equation by 3, and subtracted (in either order).

(4) There are several other ways to solve the system of equations (for example, by substitution, Gauss-Jordan reduction, or graphically), but in this case the elimination method is the fastest.

$$C = 0.25(t - f) + p$$

71. A phone company charges a fixed monthly cost, plus 25 cents per minute, after a certain number of minutes which are free. The equation above, where $p > 0$ and $t > f$, gives the total monthly cost, C, for a person that uses t minutes, based on the phone company charging a monthly fee of p dollars, and giving f minutes for free. Based on the equation, if the phone company charges a fixed cost of 40 dollars per month, and Joseph is billed $52 for using 620 minutes in October, how many minutes does the phone company give for free each month?

* We are given that $p = 40$, $C = 52$, and $t = 620$. We now solve the following equation for f.

82

$$52 = 0.25(620 - f) + 40$$
$$12 = 0.25(620 - f)$$
$$\frac{12}{0.25} = 620 - f$$
$$12 \cdot 4 = 620 - f$$
$$48 = 620 - f$$
$$-572 = -f$$
$$f = \mathbf{572}$$

Notes: (1) To get from the first equation to the second equation, we subtracted 40 from each side.

(2) To get from the second equation to the third equation, we divided each side by 0.25.

(3) If we can use a calculator for this problem, we would simply divide 12 by 0.25 in our calculator by typing 12 /.25 ENTER. The display would then show 48.

If we cannot use a calculator, we could divide 12 by 0.25 as follows.

$$\frac{12}{0.25} = 12 \div \frac{1}{4} = 12 \cdot 4 = 48$$

(4) To get from the fifth equation to the sixth equation, we subtracted 620 from each side.

(5) To get from the sixth equation to the last equation, we negated each side of the equation, or equivalently, we multiplied each side of the equation by -1.

72. If $(x^{2y})^z = \dfrac{x^{w^2}}{x^{v^2}}$, $x > 1$, $2yz = w - v$, and $w \neq v$, what is the value of $w + v$?

* $(x^{2y})^z = x^{2yz}$ and $\dfrac{x^{w^2}}{x^{v^2}} = x^{w^2 - v^2}$. So $w - v = 2yz = w^2 - v^2$. We can factor $w^2 - v^2$ as $(w + v)(w - v)$. Thus, $w - v = (w + v)(w - v)$. Therefore, $w + v = \dfrac{w-v}{w-v} = \mathbf{1}$.

Note: For the laws of exponents used here, see the table below.

For example, we used the law $(x^a)^b = x^{ab}$ to get

83

$$(x^{2y})^z = x^{(2y)z} = x^{2yz}.$$

Similarly, we used the law $\dfrac{x^a}{x^b} = x^{a-b}$ to get

$$\frac{x^{w^2}}{x^{v^2}} = x^{w^2-v^2}.$$

Laws of Exponents: For those students that have forgotten, here is a brief review of the laws of exponents.

Law	Example
$x^0 = 1$	$3^0 = 1$
$x^1 = x$	$9^1 = 9$
$x^a x^b = x^{a+b}$	$x^3 x^5 = x^8$
$x^a/x^b = x^{a-b}$	$x^{11}/x^4 = x^7$
$(x^a)^b = x^{ab}$	$(x^5)^3 = x^{15}$
$(xy)^a = x^a y^a$	$(xy)^4 = x^4 y^4$
$(x/y)^a = x^a/y^a$	$(x/y)^6 = x^6/y^6$
$x^{-1} = 1/x$	$3^{-1} = 1/3$
$x^{-a} = 1/x^a$	$9^{-2} = 1/81$
$x^{1/n} = \sqrt[n]{x}$	$x^{1/3} = \sqrt[3]{x}$
$x^{m/n} = \sqrt[n]{x^m} = \left(\sqrt[n]{x}\right)^m$	$x^{9/2} = \sqrt{x^9} = \left(\sqrt{x}\right)^9$

LEVEL 3: GEOMETRY AND TRIG

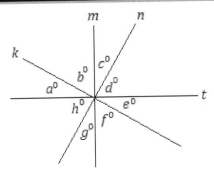

Note: Figure not drawn to scale.

73. In the figure above, lines k, m, n, and t intersect at a point. If $a + b + c = f + g + h$, which of the following must be true?

I. $d = e$
II. $a + b = f + h$
III. $b + c = g + h$

(A) I and II only
(B) I and III only
(C) II and III only
(D) I, II, and III

* **Complete geometric solution:** Since t is a straight line, we have both $a + b + c + d = 180$ and $e + f + g + h = 180$. So

$$a + b + c + d = e + f + g + h$$

Since $a + b + c = f + g + h$, we can substitute:

$$f + g + h + d = e + f + g + h$$

Subtracting $f + g + h$ from each side of this last equation yields $d = e$.

So I is true, and we can eliminate choice C.

Since the angles with measures c and g are vertical, they have the same measure. So $c = g$. We can therefore substitute c for g in the given equation $a + b + c = f + g + h$ to get $a + b + g = f + g + h$. Subtracting g from each side of this last equation yields $a + b = f + h$. So II is true, and we can eliminate choice B.

85

If we let $a = e = 65, b = f = 30, c = g = 20$, and $d = h = 65$, then we have

$$a + b + c + d = e + f + g + h = 180.$$

We also have

$$a + b + c = f + g + h = 115, b + c = 50, \text{ and } g + h = 85.$$

So III is false, and the answer is choice A.

Notes: (1) A pair of intersecting lines form **vertical angles**. Vertical angles are congruent (they have the same measure).

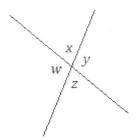

In the above figure there are two pairs of vertical angles. Angles x and z form a pair of vertical angles, and angles y and w form another pair of vertical angles. It follows that $m\angle x = m\angle z$ and $m\angle y = m\angle w$.

(2) In this problem, there are four obvious pairs of vertical angles, leading to the following true equations:

$$a = e, b = f, c = g, d = h$$

There are also other pairs of vertical angles, but we don't need those to solve the problem (as one example, we have $a + b = e + f$).

(3) A straight line consists of $180°$. So, for example, since t is a straight line, we must have $a + b + c + d = 180$.

There are four straight lines in the given figure. This leads to eight equations similar to the one we just wrote down. As a simple exercise, you may want to write out these eight equations.

(4) If you are trying to solve this problem by picking numbers (which might prove a little tricky here), be careful to notice that there are several equations that are not explicitly written in the question itself. Altogether, there are seven equations that must be satisfied:

$$a = e, b = f, c = g, d = h$$

$$a + b + c + d = 180$$

$$e + f + g + h = 180$$

$$a + b + c = f + g + h$$

The first four equations follow from notes (1) and (2), the next two from note (3), and the last one is given in the question.

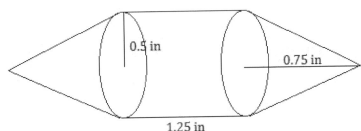

1.25 in

74. * A small capsule is created from two congruent right circular cones and a right circular cylinder with measurements shown in the figure above. Of the following, which is closest to the volume of the capsule, in cubic inches?

(A) 0.39
(B) 0.98
(C) 1.18
(D) 1.37

* The volume is

$$V = \pi(0.5)^2 \cdot 1.25 + 2\left(\frac{1}{3}\right)\pi(0.5)^2 \cdot 0.75 \approx 1.37$$

This is choice D.

Notes: (1) The capsule consists of a cylinder and two cones. We get the volume of the capsule by adding up the volumes of the three individual solids.

(2) The formulas for the volume of a cylinder and the volume of a cone are given in the beginning of each math section on the SAT. It's nice to have these formulas memorized if possible, but they are there for you if you forget them.

(3) The volume of a cylinder is $V = \pi r^2 h$, where r is the radius of each circular base of the cylinder and h is the height of the cylinder.

In this problem, the radius of a base is $r = 0.5$ and the height is $h = 1.25$. Therefore, the volume of the cylinder is

$$V = \pi(0.5)^2 \cdot 1.25 \approx 0.98.$$

(4) The volume of a cone is $V = \frac{1}{3}\pi r^2 h$, where r is the radius of the circular base of the cone and h is the height of the cone.

In this problem, the radius of the base is $r = 0.5$ and the height is $h = 0.75$. Therefore, the volume of the cone is

$$V = \frac{1}{3}\pi(0.5)^2 \cdot 0.75 \approx 0.196.$$

(5) To get the total volume of the capsule, we add the volume of the cylinder and the volume of the two cones to get approximately

$$0.98 + 2 \cdot 0.196 \approx 1.372$$

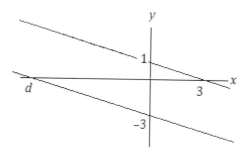

75.   In the xy-plane above, the two lines are parallel. What is the value of d ?

(A) -7
(B) -8
(C) -9
(D) -10

* Geometric solution: To get from the y-intercept to the x-intercept of the higher line, we need to go down 1, then right 3. It follows that the slope of that line is $-\frac{1}{3}$.

Similarly, the slope of the lower line is $\frac{3}{d}$

Since the two lines are parallel, they have the same slope. Therefore, we have $\frac{3}{d} = -\frac{1}{3}$.

Cross multiplying gives us $d = -9$, choice C.

Notes: (1) Slope $= \frac{\text{Rise}}{\text{Run}}$. The "rise" is the number of units we move up or down, and the "run" is the number of units we move right as we go from one point on the line to another point on the line. If we move up the slope is positive, and if we move down the slope in negative.

The following picture shows the rise and run for each line.

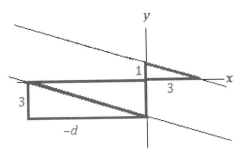

Keep in mind that d is a negative number (because it is on the negative x-axis). It follows that we should use $-d$ for the "run."

So we have that the slope of the lower line is $-\frac{3}{-d} = \frac{3}{d}$.

Algebraic solution: The higher line passes through the points $(0, 1)$ and $(3, 0)$. Therefore, the slope of that line is $\frac{0-1}{3-0} = -\frac{1}{3}$

The lower line passes through the points $(0, -3)$ and $(d, 0)$. Therefore, the slope of that line is $\frac{-3-0}{0-d} = \frac{-3}{-d} = \frac{3}{d}$.

Since parallel lines have the same slope, we have $-\frac{1}{3} = \frac{3}{d}$.

Cross multiplying gives us $d = -9$, choice C.

Note: See problem 16 for more information on slope.

76. The graph of the linear function g has intercepts at $(c, 0)$ and $(0, c)$ in the xy-plane. If $c \neq 0$ which of the following is true about the slope of the graph of g ?

(A) It is zero.
(B) It is positive.
(C) It is negative.
(D) It is undefined.

Solution by picking a number: Let's choose a value for c, say $c = 2$. Then the line passes through the points $(2, 0)$ and $(0, 2)$. So the slope of the line is $m = \frac{2-0}{0-2} = \frac{2}{-2} = -1$. We see that the slope is negative, choice C.

Note: See problem 16 for more information on slope (including the slope formula).

(2) Instead of using the slope formula we can plot the two points, draw the line passing through them, and observe that the line is moving downward from left to right.

* Direct solution: The slope of the line passing through the points $(c, 0)$ and $(0, c)$ is $\frac{c-0}{0-c} = \frac{c}{-c} = -1$. We see that the slope is negative, choice C.

Note: There is very little difference between the two solutions given. Algebraically they are the same, although some students might find it easier to deal with specific points.

77. The measure x, in degrees, of an exterior angle of a regular polygon is related to the number of sides, n, of the polygon by the formula $nx = 360$. If the measure of an exterior angle of a regular polygon is less than $80°$, what is the least number of sides it can have?

* We are given $x < 80$, so that $\frac{1}{x} > \frac{1}{80}$. It follows that

$$n = \frac{360}{x} = 360 \left(\frac{1}{x}\right) > 360 \left(\frac{1}{80}\right) = 4.5.$$

So the least possible value for n is **5.**

78. The graph of a line in the (x, y)-plane passes through the points $(2, 3)$ and $(3, 4)$. The graph of a second line has slope 3 and contains the point $(1, 5)$. If the two lines intersect at the point (x, y), what is the value of $1 - xy$?

* The slope of the first line is $m = \frac{4-3}{3-2} = \frac{1}{1} = 1$. Using the point $(2, 3)$, we can write an equation of the line in point-slope form as

$$y - 3 = 1(x - 2), \text{ or equivalently } y = x + 1.$$

We can write an equation of the second line in point-slope form as

$y - 5 = 3(x - 1)$, or equivalently $y = 3x + 2$.

Since both equations have y by itself, let's solve the system of equations using the *substitution method.*

We have $x + 1 = 3x + 2$, or equivalently $2x = -1$. So $x = -\frac{1}{2}$.

It follows that $y = x + 1 = -\frac{1}{2} + 1 = \frac{1}{2}$.

Therefore, $1 - xy = 1 - \left(-\frac{1}{2}\right)\left(\frac{1}{2}\right) = 1 + \frac{1}{4} = 5/4$ or 1.25.

Notes: (1) See problem 16 for more information on slope and see problem 41 for more information on the slope-intercept form of an equation of a line.

(2) The **point-slope form of an equation of a line** is

$$y - y_0 = m(x - x_0)$$

where m is the slope of the line and (x_0, y_0) is any point on the line.

(3) We can change a line from point-slope form to slope-intercept form simply by solving the equation for y.

For example, the equation $y - 5 = 3(x - 1)$ is in point-slope form. We distribute the 3 to get $y - 5 = 3x - 3$. Then we add 5 to each side of the equation to get $y = 3x + 2$. This last equation is now in slope-intercept form.

(4) We needed to solve the system of equations

$$y = x + 1$$
$$y = 3x + 2$$

In the above solution we chose to use the *substitution method.* Since y is equal to both $x + 1$ and $3x + 2$, we must have these two quantities equal to each other.

(5) We can also solve the system of equations by using the *elimination method.* One way to do this is to multiply the first equation by -1 and then add the two equations.

$$-1 \cdot y = (x + 1)(-1)$$
$$y = 3x + 2$$

91

$$-y = -x - 1$$
$$y = 3x + 2$$
$$0 = 2x + 1$$

Solving this last equation for x gives us $x = -\frac{1}{2}$ (just like in the above solution).

79. In a circle with center O, central angle POQ has a measure of $\frac{5\pi}{6}$ radians. The area of the sector formed by central angle POQ is what fraction of the area of the circle?

* One full rotation is 2π radians, and $\frac{5\pi}{6} \div 2\pi = \frac{5\pi}{6} \cdot \frac{1}{2\pi} = \textbf{5/12}$.

Notes: (1) We can also grid in one of the decimals $.\textbf{416}$ or $.\textbf{417}$.

(2) We can also change $\frac{5\pi}{6}$ to degrees first: $\frac{5\pi}{6} = \frac{5(180)}{6} = 150°$.

We then have $\frac{150}{360} = \textbf{5/12}$.

Quick lesson in degree and radian measure: One full rotation of a circle is 360°. All other rotations are in proportion to the full rotation. For example, half of a rotation of a circle is $\frac{360}{2} = 180°$.

In addition to degree measure, another way to measure rotations of a circle is to divide the arc length of the circle by the radius of the circle. This is called **radian** measure. For example, one full rotation of a circle is $\frac{2\pi r}{r} = 2\pi$ radians, and so half of a rotation of a circle is π radians.

So, we just showed that $180° = \pi$ radians.

We can convert between degree measure and radian measure by using the following simple ratio:

$$\frac{\text{degree measure}}{180°} = \frac{\text{radian measure}}{\pi}$$

Example 1: Convert 45° to radians.

Solution: $\frac{45°}{180°} = \frac{x}{\pi} \Rightarrow x = \frac{45\pi}{180} = \frac{\pi}{4}$ radians.

Shortcut: We can convert from degrees to radians by multiplying the given angle by $\frac{\pi}{180}$.

Example 2: Convert $\frac{\pi}{6}$ radians to degrees.

Solution: $\frac{x°}{180°} = \frac{\pi/6}{\pi} \Rightarrow x = \frac{180}{6} = \mathbf{30°}.$

Shortcut: We can convert from radians to degrees by multiplying the given angle by $\frac{180}{\pi}$.

If the angle has π in the numerator, we can simply replace π by 180.

80. In a right triangle, one angle measures $\theta°$, where $\cos\theta° = \frac{3}{5}$. What is $\sin((90-\theta)°)$

* Solution using a cofunction identity: $\sin((90-\theta)°) = \cos\theta° = 3/5$ or .**6**.

Note: It's worth memorizing the following two cofunction identities:

$$\sin(90° - x) = \cos x \qquad\qquad \cos(90° - x) = \sin x$$

Basic trig solution: Let's draw a picture:

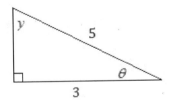

Notice that I labeled one of the angles with θ, and used the fact that $\cos\theta = \frac{\text{ADJ}}{\text{HYP}}$ to label 2 sides of the triangle.

Now observe that $y° = (90-\theta)°$, so that

$$\sin((90-\theta)°) = \sin y° = \frac{\text{OPP}}{\text{HYP}} = 3/5 \text{ or } .6.$$

Note: See problem 12 for the basic trigonometry used here.

LEVEL 3: PASSPORT TO ADVANCED MATH

Questions 81 - 82 refer to the following information.

The complete graph of the function g is shown in the xy-plane below.

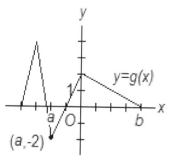

81. For what value of x is the value of $g(x)$ at its maximum?

    (A) -3
    (B) -2
    (C) 0
    (D) 4

* Let's just point out the maximum value of $g(x)$, emphasizing the x-value at which it occurs.

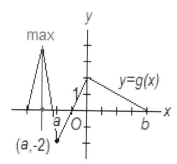

Simply note that the maximum occurs at $x = -3$, choice A.

Note: The maximum value (which is a y-value) is $y = 4$, but the place where this maximum occurs (which is an x-value) is $x = -3$.

82. Which of the following are equal to 2 ?

  I. $g(-4)$
  II. $g(0)$
  III. $g(b) - g(a)$

  (A) II only
  (B) I and III only
  (C) II and III only
  (D) I, II, and III

* The point $(-4, 0)$ is on the graph of g. Therefore, $g(-4) = 0 \neq 2$. So we can eliminate choices B and D.

The points $(a, -2)$ and $(b, 0)$ are on the graph of g. Thus, $g(a) = -2$ and $g(b) = 0$. So $g(b) - g(a) = 0 - (-2) = 0 + 2 = 2$. So the answer is choice C.

Notes: (1) If f is a function, then

  $f(a) = b$ is equivalent to "the point (a, b) lies on the graph of f."

(2) The first paragraph of the solution tells us that I does not work. So we can eliminate each choice with a I in it. This is why we can eliminate choices B and D.

(3) It might seem natural to try II next. But there is actually no need to since both of the remaining choices have II in them.

So we skip right to III.

(4) The last paragraph of the solution tells us that III works. Since choice A does NOT have III in it, we can eliminate it. This leaves only choice C.

(5) For completeness, let's look at II (this is not necessary to complete the problem, but it can be used as an additional check). The point $(0, 2)$ is on the graph of g. Therefore, $g(0) = 2$. So we can eliminate choice B.

83. Which of the following is equivalent to the expression $x^3y^2 - xy^2 + 2x^2 - 2$?

  (A) $xy^2(x^2 - 1) + 2x(x - 2)$
  (B) $(xy^2 + 2)(x^2 - 1)$
  (C) $(xy + y)(x - 2)$
  (D) $xy^2(x^2 + 2 - y)$

Solution by picking numbers: Let's choose values for x and y. In this case let's try $x = y = 0$. Then $x^3y^2 - xy^2 + 2x^2 - 2 = -2$.

Put a nice big dark circle around -2 so you can find it easier later. We now substitute $x = y = 0$ into each answer choice:

(A) $0 + 0 = 0$
(B) $(0 + 2)(0 - 1) = (2)(-1) = -2$
(C) $(0 + 0)(0 - 2) = 0(-2) = 0$
(D) 0

Since A, C, and D each came out incorrect, the answer is choice B.

Notes: (1) B is **not** the correct answer simply because it is equal to -2. It is correct because all three of the other choices are **not** -2. **You absolutely must check all four choices!**

(2) Usually I recommend picking a different number for each variable because we are less likely to get more than one answer choice to come out to the correct answer this way. I also usually recommend picking numbers that are simple, but not too simple. In particular, I would normally avoid picking 0 or 1. In this case, however, picking larger numbers would make the computations very tedious. So it's worth using 0 to eliminate as many choices as possible. Luckily things worked out really well and we actually managed to eliminate three of the four choices.

(3) When using the strategy of picking numbers, it is very important that we check every answer choice. It is possible for more than one choice to come out to the correct answer. We would then need to pick new numbers to try to eliminate all but one choice.

* **Solution by factoring:** We use the method of factoring by grouping.

$$x^3y^2 - xy^2 + 2x^2 - 2$$
$$= xy^2(x^2 - 1) + 2(x^2 - 1)$$
$$= (xy^2 + 2)(x^2 - 1)$$

This is choice B.

Notes: (1) Notice that the first two terms factor as

$$x^3y^2 - xy^2 = xy^2(x^2 - 1)$$

and the last two terms factor as

$$2x^2 - 2 = 2(x^2 - 1)$$

So we have
$$x^3y^2 - xy^2 + 2x^2 - 2 = xy^2(x^2 - 1) + 2(x^2 - 1)$$

(2) The expressions $xy^2(x^2 - 1)$ and $2(x^2 - 1)$ have $(x^2 - 1)$ in common, and we can therefore factor it out of the expression
$$xy^2(x^2 - 1) + 2(x^2 - 1)$$

as was done in the solution.

(3) If you have trouble seeing why the last expression is the same as what we started with, try working backwards and multiplying instead of factoring. In other words, we have
$$(xy^2 + 2)(x^2 - 1)$$
$$= (xy^2)(x^2) - 1(xy^2) + 2(x^2) + 2(-1)$$
$$= x^3y^2 - xy^2 + 2x^2 - 2$$

I used FOIL here to multiply this out, but you can use the method for multiplying polynomials that you like best (see problem 53 for another method).

(4) We can also solve this problem by starting with the answer choices and multiplying (as we did in Note (1)) until we get
$$x^3y^2 - xy^2 + 2x^2 - 2.$$

84. In the xy-plane, which of the following is an equation of a circle with center $(3,0)$ and a radius with endpoint $(2, \frac{3}{2})$?

(A) $(x + 3)^2 + y^2 = \frac{13}{4}$

(B) $(x - 3)^2 + y^2 = \frac{13}{4}$

(C) $(x + 3)^2 + y^2 = \frac{\sqrt{13}}{2}$

(D) $(x - 3)^2 + y^2 = \frac{\sqrt{13}}{2}$

* Recall that the equation of a circle with center (h, k) and radius r is
$$(x - h)^2 + (y - k)^2 = r^2$$

In this problem, $h = 3$ and $k = 0$. So the equation is
$$(x - 3)^2 + (y - 0)^2 = r^2$$

or equivalently,

$$(x - 3)^2 + y^2 = r^2$$

This eliminates choices A and C.

Since the point $(2, \frac{3}{2})$ lies on the circle, we can plug this point in to find r^2.

$$(2 - 3)^2 + \left(\frac{3}{2}\right)^2 = (-1)^2 + \frac{9}{4} = 1 + \frac{9}{4} = \frac{4}{4} + \frac{9}{4} = \frac{13}{4}$$

So $r^2 = \frac{13}{4}$, and the answer is choice B.

Note: Be careful here. The radius of the circle is $r = \sqrt{\frac{13}{4}} = \frac{\sqrt{13}}{2}$, but the right hand side of the standard form of an equation of a circle is r^2.

85. In the xy-plane, the parabola with equation $y = (x + 7)^2$ intersects the line with equation $y = 9$ at two points, P and Q. What is the length of $\overline{PQ}$?

Solution using the square root property: Replacing y with 9 in the first equation yields $(x + 7)^2 = 9$. We use the square root property to get $x + 7 = \pm 3$. So $x = -7 \pm 3$. So the two solutions are $x = -7 + 3 = -4$ and $x = -7 - 3 = -10$.

Sp $P = (-4, 9)$ and $Q = (-10, 9)$. The distance between these two points is $|-10 - (-4)| = |-10 + 4| = |-6| = \mathbf{6}$.

Notes: (1) To find the points of intersection of the parabola and the line, we solve the given system of equations. We chose to use the **substitution method** here.

(2) Instead of formally applying the square root property to solve $(x + 7)^2 = 9$, we can simply "guess" the solutions, or solve the equation informally. It's not too hard to see that $x = -4$ and $x = -10$ will make the equation true.

(3) It's not necessary to write down the points P and Q. Since the y-coordinates of the two points are the same, we can simply subtract one from the other (disregarding the minus sign if it appears) to get the desired distance.

(4) We can also plot the two points and observe that the distance between them is 6.

86. The function g is defined by $g(x) = 5 - |x - 3|$. If $g(a) = g(1)$, and $a \neq 1$, what is the value of a ?

* $g(1) = 5 - |1 - 3| = 5 - |-2| = 5 - 2 = 3$. Since $g(a) = g(1)$, we have $g(a) = 3$. So,

$$5 - |a - 3| = 3$$
$$-|a - 3| = 3 - 5$$
$$-|a - 3| = -2$$
$$|a - 3| = 2$$

From here it is easy to see that $a = \mathbf{5}$.

Note: For completeness, here are the algebraic details for solving the equation $|a - 3| = 2$.

The absolute value equation is equivalent to the two equations

$$a - 3 = 2 \quad \text{or} \quad a - 3 = -2$$
$$a = 2 + 3 = 5 \quad \text{or} \quad a = -2 + 3 = 1$$

So the two solutions are $a = 5$ and $a = 1$.

Quick lesson in absolute value: The **absolute value** of x, written $|x|$ is simply x if x is nonnegative, and $-x$ if x is negative. Put simply, $|x|$ just removes the minus sign if one is there.

Examples: $|3| = 3$, and $|-3| = 3$. Also, $|0| = 0$.

Geometrically, $|x - y|$ is the distance between x and y. In particular, $|x - y| = |y - x|$.

Examples: $|5 - 3| = |3 - 5| = 2$ because the distance between 3 and 5 is 2.

If $|x - 3| = 7$, then the distance between x and 3 is 7. So there are two possible values for x. They are $3 + 7 = 10$, and $3 - 7 = -4$. See the figure below for clarification.

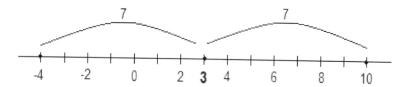

If $|x - 3| < 7$, then the distance between x and 3 is less than 7. If you look at the above figure you should be able to see that this is all x satisfying $-4 < x < 10$.

If $|x - 3| > 7$, then the distance between x and 3 is greater than 7. If you look at the above figure you should be able to see that this is all x satisfying $x < -4$ or $x > 10$.

Algebraically, we have the following. For $c > 0$,

$$|x| = c \text{ is equivalent to } x = c \text{ or } x = -c$$

$$|x| < c \text{ is equivalent to } -c < x < c$$

$$|x| > c \text{ is equivalent to } x < -c \text{ or } x > c.$$

Let's look at the same examples as before algebraically.

Examples: If $|x - 3| = 7$, then $x - 3 = 7$ or $x - 3 = -7$. So $x = 10$ or $x = -4$.

If $|x - 3| < 7$, then $-7 < x - 3 < 7$. So $-4 < x < 10$.

If $|x - 3| > 7$, then $x - 3 < -7$ or $x - 3 > 7$. So $x < -4$ or $x > 10$.

87. In the xy-plane, the point $(-2, 5)$ lies on the graph of the function $h(x) = 2x^2 - kx + 7$. What is the value of $1 - k$?

* **Solution:** Since the point $(-2, 5)$ lies on the graph of h, we have $h(-2) = 5$. But by direct computation

$$h(-2) = 2(-2)^2 - k(-2) + 7 = 2 \cdot 4 + 2k + 7$$
$$= 8 + 2k + 7 = 15 + 2k.$$

So $15 + 2k = 5$. Therefore, $2k = -10$, and so $k = -5$.

Finally, we have $1 - k = 1 - (-5) = 1 + 5 = $ **6**.

Note: If f is a function, then

$f(a) = b$ is equivalent to "the point (a, b) lies on the graph of f."

100

$$h = -5t^2 + 16t$$

88. The equation above expresses the approximate height h, in meters, of an arrow t seconds after it is shot into the air with an initial velocity of 16 meters per second. After how many seconds will the arrow hit the ground?

* The arrow hits the ground when the height of the arrow is 0. So we set $h = 0$, or equivalently, $-5t^2 + 16t = 0$.

We now solve for t.

$$-5t^2 + 16t = 0$$
$$t(-5t + 16) = 0$$

$t = 0$ or $-5t + 16 = 0$

$t = 0$ or $-5t = -16$

$t = 0$ or $t = \dfrac{-16}{-5} = \dfrac{16}{5}$

So we can grid in **16/5** or **3.2**.

Notes: (1) Although $t = 0$ is a solution to the equation $-5t^2 + 16t = 0$, it is not an acceptable answer because the arrow was launched at time $t = 0$, whereas we are looking for when the arrow hit the ground (after it was launched). Clearly the arrow hits the ground after time 0.

(2) Based on the last note, after factoring, we can disregard the equation $t = 0$ and simply solve the equation $-5t + 16 = 0$.

LEVEL 3: PROBLEM SOLVING AND DATA

Questions 89 - 90 refer to the following information.

Bethany went shopping at a clothing store; the items she purchased are shown below.

Details

7 Shirts

5 Dresses

11 Hats

Sales Tax Paid $31.37

Grand Total $479.54

The sales tax is calculated as a percentage of the cost of Bethany's purchase. The grand total is the sum of the cost of Bethany's purchase and the sales tax.

89.   * Approximately what percentage of the cost of Bethany's purchase was used to calculate the sales tax?

   (A) 7%
   (B) 9%
   (C) 11%
   (D) 13%

Solution by starting with choice C: The total *before* sales tax was $479.54 - 31.37 = 448.17$.

We start with choice C and guess that the sales tax is 11%. The grand total would then be $1.11 \cdot 448.17 \approx 497.47$. This is too big, and so we can eliminate choices C and D.

Let's try B next and guess that the sales tax was 9%. The grand total would then be $1.09 \cdot 448.17 \approx 488.51$. This is still too big, and so we can eliminate choice B. The answer must therefore be choice A.

Notes: (1) There are two ways to increase 448.17 by 11%.

Method 1: We can take 11% of 448.17, and then add the result to 448.17:

$$0.11 \cdot 448.17 \approx 49.30 \text{ and } 448.17 + 49.30 = 497.47.$$

<u>Method 2</u>: Note that increasing 448.17 by 11% is the same as taking 111% of 448.17:

$$1.11 \cdot 448.17 \approx 497.47.$$

(2) To see that Methods 1 and 2 lead to the same answer, note that

$$448.17 + 0.11 \cdot 448.17 = (1 + 0.11) \cdot 448.17 = 1.11 \cdot 448.17$$

Similarly, we can use either of these methods with the other answer choices.

(3) For completeness, let's check that choice A gives the desire result. Let's use Method 2 since it's quicker:

$$1.07 \cdot 448.17 \approx 479.54$$

* Direct solution: $\frac{31.37}{479.54} \approx 0.0654169 \approx 0.07 = 7\%$, choice A.

Notes: (1) To compute a percentage, use the simple formula

$$Percentage = \frac{Part}{Whole} \times 100$$

In this problem the *Part* is the sales tax and the *Whole* is the grand total. So we get $\frac{31.37}{479.54} \times 100 \approx 7\%$.

(2) Alternatively we can simply divide the *Part* by the *Whole* and then change the resulting decimal to a percent by moving the decimal point to the right two places. This is how we did it in the direct solution above.

Algebraic solution: We want to answer the question "31.37 is what percent of 479.54?" We replace "is" by "=," we replace "what percent" by "$\frac{x}{100}$," we replace "of" by "$\cdot$," and we solve the resulting equation for x.

$$31.37 = \frac{x}{100} \cdot 479.54$$

$$31.37 \cdot \frac{100}{479.54} = x$$

$$x \approx 6.54 \approx 7$$

This is choice A.

90. * The total amount Bethany paid for shirts and dresses was $324.31. If the combined cost of one shirt and one dress is $55.59, what is the cost of one shirt?

    (A) $11.26
    (B) $23.18
    (C) $32.41
    (D) $37.85

Solution by starting with choice C: We start with choice C and guess that the cost of one shirt is $32.41. It follows that the cost of one dress is $55.59 - 32.41 = 23.18$ dollars, and so the total cost for shirts and dresses was $7 \cdot 32.41 + 5 \cdot 23.18 = 342.77$ dollars. This is too big and so we can eliminate choice C.

Let's try B next and guess that the cost of one shirt is $23.18. It follows that the cost of one dress is $55.59 - 23.18 = 32.41$ dollars, and so the total cost for shirts and dresses was $7 \cdot 23.18 + 5 \cdot 32.41 = 324.31$ dollars. This is correct. So the answer is B.

Note: Don't forget to look back at the information you were given for this question. We needed that information to solve the problem. In particular, we needed to know that Bethany purchased 7 shirts and 5 dresses.

* Solution using the elimination method: Let's let s be the cost of one shirt, in dollars, and d be the cost of one dress, in dollars. Then the total amount Bethany paid for shirts and dresses was $7s + 5d$, and we are given that this is equal to 324.31 dollars.

The cost of one shirt and one dress is $s + d$, and we are given that this is equal to 55.59 dollars.

So we have the following system of equations:

$$7s + 5d = 324.31$$
$$s + d = 55.59$$

We will now multiply each side of the second equation by -5.

$$7s + 5d = 324.31$$
$$-5(s + d) = 55.59(-5)$$

Do not forget to distribute correctly on the left. Then add the two equations.

$$7s + 5d = 324.31$$
$$-5s - 5d = -277.95$$
$$2s = 46.36$$

We divide each side of this last equation by 2 to get $s = \frac{46.36}{2} = 23.18$ dollars, choice B.

Notes: (1) We chose to multiply the second equation by -5 because multiplying by this number makes the d column "match up" so that when we add the two equations in the next step the d term vanishes.

(2) If we wanted to find d instead of s we would multiply the second equation by -7. In general, if you are looking for only one variable, try to eliminate the one you are **not** looking for.

(3) We chose to multiply by a negative number so that we could add the equations instead of subtracting them. We could have also multiplied the second equation by 5, and subtracted the second equation from the first.

(4) There are several other ways to solve the system of equations (for example, by substitution, Gauss-Jordan reduction, or graphically), but in this case the elimination method is the fastest.

$$P = mgh$$

91. The potential energy of an object can be calculated using the formula above, where P is the potential energy of the object in joules, m is the mass of the object in kilograms, g is the acceleration due to gravity (approximately 9.8 meters per second per second), and h is the height of the object in meters. Which of the following is closest to ten joules?

(A) The potential energy of an object with a mass of $\frac{1}{2}$ kilogram and a height of 1 meter
(B) The potential energy of an object with a mass of $\frac{1}{2}$ kilogram and a height of 2 meters
(C) The potential energy of an object with a mass of 1 kilogram and a height of $\frac{1}{2}$ meter
(D) The potential energy of an object with a mass of 1 kilogram and a height of 2 meters

* **Solution by plugging in each answer choice:** Let's evaluate P for each answer choice and see which one comes closest to 10.

(A) $P \approx \frac{1}{2} \cdot 9.8 \cdot 1 = 4.9$

(B) $P \approx \frac{1}{2} \cdot 9.8 \cdot 2 = 9.8$

(C) $P \approx 1 \cdot 9.8 \cdot \frac{1}{2} = 4.9$

(D) $P \approx 1 \cdot 9.8 \cdot 2 = 19.6$

Since 9.8 is the closest to 10, the answer is choice B.

Types of animals	Percent in pet store
Mammal	15%
Bird	8%
Reptile	25%
Amphibian	12%
Fish	40%

92. * The table above shows the distribution of the five types of animals in a pet store. If there are 60 more fish than mammals, how many animals are in the pet store?

(A) 120
(B) 200
(C) 240
(D) 400

Solution by starting with choice C: We start with choice C and guess that the number of animals in the pet store is 240.

Since 15% of the animals are mammals, there are $0.15 \cdot 240 = 36$ mammals in the pet store.

Since 40% of the animals are fish, there are $0.40 \cdot 240 = 96$ fish in the pet store.

Now, $96 - 36 = 60$, and so there are 60 more fish than mammals. This is correct, and so the answer is C.

* Algebraic solution: If we let m be the number of mammals, then the number of fish is $m + 60$.

If we let t be the total number of animals in the pet store, then we have $0.15t = m$ and $0.40t = m + 60$. If we subtract the first equation from the second, we get

$$0.40t = m + 60$$
$$\underline{0.15t = m}$$
$$0.25t = 60$$

We divide each side of this last equation by 0.25 to get $t = \frac{60}{0.25} = 240$, choice C.

Questions 93 - 94 refer to the following information.

Annual Expenses for a Fitness Center, 2011-2014				
	2011	**2012**	**2013**	**2014**
Rent	380	410	425	438
Utilities	36	37.5	38.25	40.1
Advertising	80	72	90.5	120.5
Insurance	30	32	35	37.5
Legal	52	57	68	64

The table above lists the money spent annually by a fitness center, in hundreds of dollars, on each of five expenses from 2011 to 2014.

93. * Of the following, which ratio of the expense in 2014 to the same expense in 2011 is closest to the rent expense's ratio in 2014 to the rent expense's ratio in 2011 ?

   (A) Utilities
   (B) Advertising
   (C) Insurance
   (D) Legal

* Let's compute all five ratios.

Rent	$438 \div 380 \approx 1.15$
Utilities	$40.1 \div 36 \approx 1.11$
Advertising	$120.5 \div 80 \approx 1.51$
Insurance	$37.5 \div 30 = 1.25$
Legal	$64 \div 52 \approx 1.23$

The closest of the last four numbers to 1.15 is 1.11. This is the ratio for Utilities, choice A.

Notes: (1) $1.15 - 1.11 = 0.04$ and $1.23 - 1.15 = 0.08$

The first difference is smaller ($0.04 < 0.08$), and so the answer is Utilities.

(2) We do not need to check B and C because the corresponding ratios are larger than 1.23.

(3) Since the entries in the table are in hundreds of dollars, technically we should be multiplying each table entry by 100 before performing the division. But we do not need to actually do this because the ratios will come out the same.

For example, $43,800 \div 38,000 = 438 \div 380$.

94. Find the average rate of change per year in the legal expense for the fitness center from 2011 to 2014.

* Quick computation: $\dfrac{6400-5200}{2014-2011} = \dfrac{1200}{3} = \mathbf{400}$.

Notes: (1) The **average rate of change** of a function is the ratio of the change in the dependent variable to the change in the independent variable.

$$\text{Average Rate of Change} = \frac{\text{change in dependent variable}}{\text{change in independent variable}} = \frac{y_2 - y_1}{x_2 - x_1}$$

In this question, the independent variable is changing from 2011 to 2014, and the dependent variable is changing from 5200 to 6400.

(2) We can also think of the average rate of change as the slope of the line passing through the points (x_1, y_1) and (x_2, y_2).

In this problem, the two points are $(2011, 5200)$ and $(2014, 6400)$, and we have

$$\text{Slope} = \frac{y_2 - y_1}{x_2 - x_1} = \frac{6400 - 5200}{2014 - 2011} = \frac{1200}{3} = \mathbf{400}$$

Questions 95 - 96 refer to the following information.

Markus opened a savings account that earns 1.4 percent interest compounded annually. His initial deposit was \$450, and he uses the expression $\$450(1 + r)^t$ to find the value of the account after t years.

95. What is the value of r in the expression?

* **Solution by picking a number:** Let's let $t = 1$. After 1 year, the interest earned on \$450 is $0.014 \cdot 450 = \$6.30$. Therefore, the amount in the account after 1 year is $450 + 6.30 = \$456.30$.

So we have $456.30 = 450(1 + r)^1$. We divide each side of this last equation by 450 to get $1 + r = \frac{456.30}{450} = 1.014$. So we have

$$r = 1.014 - 1 = .014$$

96. * Markus's sister Catelyn opened a savings account that earns 1.9 percent interest compounded annually. Catelyn also made an initial deposit of \$450 into this account at the same time that Markus made his initial deposit of \$450. After 15 years, how much more money will Catelyn's initial deposit have earned than Markus's initial deposit? (Round your answer to the nearest cent and ignore the dollar sign when gridding your response.)

* $450(1.019)^{15} - 450(1.014)^{15} \approx 42.44795951$. When we round this to the nearest cent (and ignore the dollar sign), we get **42.45**.

Notes: (1) In the last problem we found that if the interest rate is 1.4, then $r = 0.014$, and so the formula becomes

$$450(1 + 0.014)^t = 450(1.014)^t$$

(2) A similar computation shows that if the interest rate is 1.9, then $r = 0.019$, and the formula becomes

$$450(1 + 0.019)^t = 450(1.019)^t$$

(3) The question is asking for the difference between these two expressions when $t = 15$ (after 15 years). So we replace t by 15 in each expression, and then subtract.

Level 4: Heart of Algebra

$$y = (x + 7)(3x - 5)$$
$$x = 3y + 1$$

97. How many ordered pairs (x, y) satisfy the system of equations shown above?

    (A) None
    (B) One
    (C) Two
    (D) More than two

Solution by substitution: We replace x by $3y + 1$ twice in the right hand side of the first equation to get

$$y = (3y + 8)(9y - 2) = 27y^2 + 66y - 16$$

Subtracting y from each side of this last equation yields

$$0 = 27y^2 + 65y - 16$$

This is a quadratic equation with $a = 27$, $b = 65$, and $c = -16$. We compute the discriminant of this equation to get

$$b^2 - 4ac = 65^2 - 4(27)(-16) = 65^2 + 4(27)(16) > 0$$

Since the discriminant is positive, the quadratic equation has **two** real solutions, choice C.

Notes: (1) Recall that the quadratic equation $ax^2 + bx + c = 0$ can be solved by using the quadratic formula

$$x = \frac{-b \pm \sqrt{b^2 - 4ac}}{2a}$$

The quantity under the square root, $b^2 - 4ac$, is called the *discriminant* of the quadratic equation. If the discriminant is positive, then the equation has 2 real solutions. If the discriminant is zero, then the equation has 1 real solution. And if the discriminant is negative, then the equation has no real solutions (the solutions are complex in this case).

(2) It was not necessary to finish computing the discriminant in this problem. We needed only to find out if it was positive, zero, or negative.

(3) Since the equation $x = 3y + 1$ is linear, each y-value leads to a unique x-value. Since there are exactly two y-values satisfying the system of equations, there are exactly two points that are solutions to the system of equations.

* Quick graphical solution: We can get a quick rough sketch of the parabola by plotting the two x-intercepts $(-7, 0)$ and $(\frac{5}{3}, 0)$ and noting that the parabola opens upwards.

We can then plot the x-intercept of the line, $(1, 0)$ and note that the slope of the line is $m = \frac{1}{3}$. A quick sketch will show that the line hits the parabola twice.

Notes: (1) To see that the slope of the line is $\frac{1}{3}$, we need to solve the second equation for y to get $y = \frac{1}{3}x - \frac{1}{3}$.

(2) If a calculator were allowed for this problem, we could also solve it by graphing the two equations in our calculator, finding an appropriate window, and counting the points of intersection. Note that we would first have to solve the second equation for y. I leave the details of this solution to the reader.

$$2x + 5 + k = 7x$$
$$2y + 5 + t = 7y$$

98. In the equations above, k and t are constants. If t is k minus $\frac{1}{3}$, which of the following is true?

(A) x is y minus $\frac{1}{3}$.

(B) x is y minus $\frac{1}{15}$

(C) x is y plus $\frac{1}{3}$

(D) x is y plus $\frac{1}{15}$

* Solution using the elimination method: We begin by replacing t by $k - \frac{1}{3}$, and interchanging the order of the two equations.

$$2y + 5 + k - \frac{1}{3} = 7y$$
$$2x + 5 + k \phantom{- \frac{1}{3}} = 7x$$

We then subtract the bottom equation from the top equation.

$$2y - 2x - \frac{1}{3} = 7y - 7x$$

We solve this equation for x by adding $7x$, subtracting $2y$, and adding $\frac{1}{3}$ to each side of the equation,

$$5x = 5y + \frac{1}{3}$$

Finally, we multiply each side of this last equation by $\frac{1}{5}$ to get

$$x = \frac{1}{5}\left(5y + \frac{1}{3}\right) = \frac{1}{5} \cdot 5y + \frac{1}{5} \cdot \frac{1}{3} = y + \frac{1}{15}$$

So x is y plus $\frac{1}{15}$, choice D.

99. A $k\%$ acid solution is a mixture of acid and water consisting of $k\%$ acid. Martin wants to make a mixture of no more than 3 quarts from an 8% solution and a 14% solution to get a solution consisting of at least 12% acid. Let x be the number of quarts of the 8% solution, and let y be the number of quarts of the 14% solution in the mixture. Which of the following systems represents all the constraints that x and y must satisfy?

(A) $\begin{cases} 0 < x < 3 \\ 0 < y < 3 \\ \frac{8x+14y}{x+y} \geq 12 \end{cases}$

(B) $\begin{cases} x > 0 \\ y > 0 \\ x + y \leq 3 \\ 8x + 14y \geq 12(x+y) \end{cases}$

(C) $\begin{cases} x > 0 \\ y > 0 \\ x + y \leq 3 \\ 8x + 14y \geq 12 \end{cases}$

(D) $\begin{cases} x > 0 \\ y > 0 \\ x + y = 3 \\ 8x + 14y \leq 12 \end{cases}$

112

* Since x is the number of quarts of the 8% solution, y is the number of quarts of the 14% solution, and we want *no more* than 3 quarts in total, we must have $x + y \leq 3$. This narrows down our answer to either choice B or C.

Now $0.08x$ is the amount of acid in the 8% solution, $0.12y$ is the amount of acid in the 14% solution. It follows that when we mix the two together, the amount of acid will be $0.08x + 0.12y$.

We also have that the total amount of solution is $x + y$. Since we want the mixture to contain at least 12% acid, we are insisting that

$$0.08x + 0.14y \geq 0.12(x + y).$$

If we multiply each side of this last equation by 100, we get

$$8x + 14y \geq 12(x + y).$$

It follows that the answer is choice B.

Notes: (1) Since all four solutions contain the two inequalities $x > 0$ and $y > 0$, we can basically ignore them (note that choice A has these inequalities "disguised" as $0 < x$ and $0 < y$).

These two inequalities simply say that we are using a positive amount of each solution to create the mixture.

(2) The last inequality in choice in A is equivalent to the last inequality in choice B. Simply multiply each side of the inequality in A by $x + y$ to get the inequality in B (one could argue that the two inequalities are slightly different because of potential "division by zero" problems in the first inequality, but these problems do not occur because we are insisting that both $x > 0$ and $y > 0$).

(3) Multiplying a decimal by 100 is equivalent to moving the decimal point to the right two places.

For example, $100(0.08) = 8$, $100(0.14) = 14$, and $100(0.12) = 12$

(4) Make sure to use the distributive property correctly when performing the multiplication by 100 in the last step of the solution. Here are the details:

$$100(0.08x + 0.14y) \geq 100 \cdot 0.12(x + y)$$
$$100(0.08x) + 100(0.14x) \geq 12(x + y)$$
$$8x + 14y \geq 12(x + y)$$

Be careful on the right hand side of the inequality as well. The distributive property is *not* required there.

$$F = 23{,}200 - 21k$$

100. The equation above estimates the total number of fish in a lake, F, in <u>hundreds</u>, in the kth year after the year 1995. The number 21 in the equation above gives which of the following estimates?

(A) Every 21 years, there are 232 fewer fish.
(B) Every 21 years, there are 23,200 fewer fish.
(C) Every year the total number of fish in the lake decreases by 21.
(D) Every year the total number of fish in the lake decreases by 2,100.

* The given equation is linear with slope $-21 = \frac{-21}{1}$. This means that an increase in k by 1 unit corresponds to an decrease in F by 21 units. In other words, whenever the year is increased by 1, the number of fish in the lake decreases by $21 \cdot 100 = 2{,}100$, choice D.

Notes: (1) In the equation $F = 23{,}200 - 21k$, we are thinking of k as the **independent variable**, and F as the **dependent variable**. In other words, we input a value for k, and we get an F value as an output.

For example, if the input is $k = 2$ years after 1995, then the output is $F = 23{,}200 - 21 \cdot 2 = 23{,}158$. Since F is given in hundreds, we need to multiply this last number by 100 to get the number of fish in 1997. So, in 1997, there were 2,315,800 fish in the lake.

(2) Recall that the slope of a line is

$$\text{Slope} = m = \frac{\text{change in the dependent variable}}{\text{change in the independent variable}} = \frac{\text{change in } F}{\text{change in } k}$$

(3) The **slope-intercept form of an equation of a line** is $y = mx + b$ where m is the slope of the line.

The given equation can be written $F = -21K + 23{,}200$, and we see that the slope is $m = -21 = \frac{-21}{1}$.

(4) Combining notes (2) and (3), we see that a change in k by 1 unit corresponds to a change in F by 21 units.

(5) Since the sign of 21 is negative, there is a **negative association** between k and F. It follows that an increase in k corresponds to a decrease in F.

(6) Be certain to notice the underlined word <u>hundreds</u> in the question. If this wasn't there, the answer would be choice C. In this case however, when we substitute in a value for k, the corresponding F value needs to be multiplied by 100.

(7) When $k = 0$, $F = 23{,}200$. It follows that in 1995 there were 2,320,000 fish in the lake.

When $k = 1$, $F = 23{,}200 - 21 = 23{,}179$. It follows that in 1996 there were 2,317,900 fish in the lake.

From 1995 to 1996, the number of fish changed by

$$2{,}320{,}000 - 2{,}317{,}900 = 2100$$

This gives strong evidence to support choice D.

$$4x = 7 - 2y$$
$$3y - x = 9$$

101. If (x, y) is a solution to the above system of equations, what is the value of x ?

* **Solution using the elimination method:** We begin by making sure that the two equations are "lined up" properly. We do this by adding $2y$ to each side of the first equation, and interchanging the two terms on the left hand side of the second equation.

$$4x + 2y = 7$$
$$-x + 3y = 9$$

We will now multiply each side of the first equation by 3, and each side of the second equation by -2.

$$3(4x + 2y) = (7)(3)$$
$$-2(-x + 3y) = (9)(-2)$$

Do not forget to distribute correctly on the left. Add the two equations.

$$
\begin{array}{rcr}
12x + 6y &=& 21 \\
\underline{2x - 6y} &=& \underline{-18} \\
14x &=& 3
\end{array}
$$

We now divide each side of this last equation by 14 to get **3/14 or . 214**.

Remarks: (1) We chose to use 3 and -2 because multiplying by these numbers makes the y column "match up" so that when we add the two equations in the next step the y term vanishes. We could have also used -3 and 2.

(2) If we wanted to find y instead of x we would multiply only the second equation by 4. In general, if you are looking for only one variable, try to eliminate the one you are **not** looking for.

(3) We chose to multiply by a negative number so that we could add the equations instead of subtracting them. We could have also multiplied the first equation by 3, the second by 2, and subtracted the two equations, but a computational error is more likely to occur this way.

(4) This problem could be solved in several other ways such as substitution, Gauss-Jordan reduction, and graphically. I leave these alternative methods as optional exercises for the interested reader.

$$s = 35.2 + 6p$$
$$d = 45.6 - 2p$$

102. In the equations above, s and d represent the supply (the quantity supplied) and demand (the quantity demanded), in units, of a product with a price of p dollars. What is the quantity of product demanded when the supply is equal to the demand?

* **Algebraic solution:** We set s equal to d to get $35.2 + 6p = 45.6 - 2p$. We now add $2p$ to each side of the equation and subtract 35.2 from each side of the equation to get $8p = 10.4$. We divide each side of this last equation by 8 to get $p = \frac{10.4}{8} = 1.3$.

We now substitute $p = 1.3$ in to the second equation to get

$$d = 45.6 - 2 \cdot 1.3 = 45.6 - 2.6 = \mathbf{43}.$$

Note: Since $s = d$, we could also have substituted $p = 1.3$ into the first equation. We would still get an answer of 43.

103. If $x = 3\sqrt{2}$ and $4x = \sqrt{8y}$, what is the value of y ?

* Squaring each side of the equation $4x = \sqrt{8y}$ gives $16x^2 = 8y$. So we have $y = \frac{16x^2}{8} = 2x^2 = 2(3\sqrt{2})^2 = 2 \cdot 9 \cdot 2 = \mathbf{36}$.

Note: $\left(3\sqrt{2}\right)^2 = (3\sqrt{2})(3\sqrt{2}) = 3 \cdot 3 \cdot \sqrt{2} \cdot \sqrt{2} = 9 \cdot 2 = 18.$

$$\frac{1+5i}{2-3i}$$

104. If the expression above is rewritten in the form $a + bi$, where a and b are real numbers, what is the value of $b - a$?

* We multiply the numerator and denominator of $\frac{1+5i}{2-3i}$ by $(2 + 3i)$ to get

$$\frac{(1+5i)}{(2-3i)} \cdot \frac{(2+3i)}{(2+3i)} = \frac{(2-15)+(3+10)i}{4+9} = \frac{-13+13i}{13} = -\frac{13}{13} + \frac{13}{13}i = -1 + i$$

So $a = -1$, $b = 1$, and $b - a = 1 - (-1) = 1 + 1 = \mathbf{2}.$

Notes: (1) We can multiply two complex numbers by formally taking the product of two binomials and then replacing i^2 by -1.

$$(a + bi)(c + di) = (ac - bd) + (ad + bc)i$$

For example, $(1 + 5i)(2 + 3i) = (2 - 15) + (3 + 10)i = -13 + 13i$

(2) The **conjugate** of $a + bi$ is $a - bi$. The product of conjugates is always a real number. In fact,

$$(a + bi)(a - bi) = a^2 + b^2$$

For example, $(2 - 3i)(2 + 3i) = 2^2 + 3^2 = 4 + 9 = 13.$

In practice, if you forget this rule, you can simply do the multiplication formally.

(3) One way to divide two complex numbers is to multiply both the numerator and denominator by the conjugate of the denominator. This is what was done in the first equality in the solution above.

Since the product of conjugates is always a real number, this method always produces a real number in the denominator. This allows us to write the quotient in the **standard form** $a + bi$.

LEVEL 4: GEOMETRY AND TRIG

105. In the xy-plane, the line determined by the points $(c, 5)$ and $(10, 2c)$ passes through the origin. Which of the following could be the value of c ?

    (A) 0
    (B) 5
    (C) 10
    (D) 25

Solution by starting with choice B: Let's guess that $c = 5$ so that the two points are $(5, 5)$ and $(10, 10)$. It is pretty easy to see that $(0, 0)$ is on this line (see notes below). So the answer is choice B.

Notes: (1) Since $(5, 5)$ and $(10, 10)$ are both on the line, it follows that the line consists of all points for which the x and y-coordinates are equal. In particular, the origin $(0, 0)$ is on the line.

(2) Since both points have the same x and y-coordinates, the equation of the line is $y = x$. The origin $(0, 0)$ is a point on this line because $0 = 0$ is in fact true.

(3) We can formally find the slope of the line passing through $(5, 5)$ and $(10,10)$ using the slope formula: $m = \dfrac{y_2 - y_1}{x_2 - x_1} = \dfrac{10-5}{10-5} = \dfrac{5}{5} = 1.$

Alternatively, we can plot the two points and observe that to get from $(5, 5)$ to $(10, 10)$ we need to move up 5 and right 5. Thus, the slope is

$$m = \frac{rise}{run} = \frac{5}{5} = 1.$$

(4) Using the slope $m = 1$ and the point $(5, 5)$, we can write an equation of the line in point-slope form as $y - 5 = 1(x - 5)$, or equivalently $y = x$.

* Quick solution: Since we want the origin $(0, 0)$ to be on the line we must have $\dfrac{5}{c} = \dfrac{2c}{10}$. Cross multiplying gives $2c^2 = 50$. We divide each side of this last equation by 2 to get $c^2 = 25$. So $c = 5$, choice B.

Notes: (1) If the line j passes through the origin and the point (a, b) with $a \neq 0$, then the slope of line j is simply $\dfrac{b}{a}$.

So in this problem we can compute the slope as $\frac{5}{c}$ or $\frac{2c}{10}$. Since both of these quantities are equal to the slope, it follows that they are equal to each other.

(2) The equation $c^2 = 25$ actually has two solutions $c = \pm 5$. So $c = -5$ would also be an acceptable answer if it were a choice.

$$y = -\frac{3}{2}x - 5$$

106. Line k is the graph of the equation above, and line n intersects line k at the point $(-5, \frac{5}{2})$. Which of the following could be an equation of line n ?

    (A) $y = \frac{2}{3}x + 5$
    (B) $2y + 3x = 5$
    (C) $x = 8 - 2y$
    (D) $2y = x + 10$

* Solution by plugging in the point: The point $(-5, \frac{5}{2})$ lies on line n. So if we substitute $x = -5$ and $y = \frac{5}{2}$, we should get a true equation.

    (A) $\frac{5}{2} = \frac{2}{3}(-5) + 5$ $\frac{5}{2} = -\frac{10}{3} + 5$ False

    (B) $2\left(\frac{5}{2}\right) + 3(-5) = 5$ $5 - 15 = 5$ False

    (C) $-5 = 8 - 2\left(\frac{5}{2}\right)$ $-5 = 8 - 5$ False

    (D) $2\left(\frac{5}{2}\right) = -5 + 10$ $5 = 5$ True

Since only D came out true, the answer is choice D.

Notes: (1) If two lines (or any graphs for that matter) intersect at a point, that means that the point is on both lines, and so plugging that point into either equation should result in a true statement.

(2) It is true that when we plug the given point into the given equation, we do get a true statement. Indeed, we have the following:

$$\frac{5}{2} = -\frac{3}{2}(-5) - 5$$

$$\frac{5}{2} = \frac{15}{2} - \frac{10}{2}$$

$$\frac{5}{2} = \frac{5}{2}$$

It is not necessary to check this to solve the problem, however. If the problem is well written, then this will just be true.

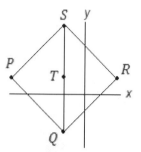

Note: Figure not drawn to scale.

107. In the xy-plane above, point T is the center of the square $PQRS$. The coordinates of points S and T are $(-2, 7)$ and $(-1, 2)$, respectively. Which of the following is an equation of the line that passes through points P and R ?

(A) $y = 2$

(B) $y = \frac{1}{5}x + 2$

(C) $y - 2 = \frac{1}{5}(x + 1)$

(D) $y - 2 = -5(x + 1)$

* The slope of the line passing through points S and T is

$$\text{Slope} = \frac{2 - 7}{-1 - (-2)} = \frac{-5}{-1 + 2} = \frac{-5}{1} = -5$$

Since the diagonals of a square are perpendicular, the slope of the line passing through points P and R is $m = \frac{1}{5}$.

So the line has a slope of $m = \frac{1}{5}$ and passes through the point $(-1, 2)$. We can therefore write an equation of the line in point-slope form as

$$y - 2 = \frac{1}{5}(x + 1).$$

This is choice C.

Notes: (1) See problem 16 for a review of slope, and problem 78 for a review of the point-slope form for the equation of a line.

(2) Perpendicular lines have slopes that are negative reciprocals of each other.

The reciprocal of $-5 = \frac{-5}{1}$ is $\frac{1}{-5} = -\frac{1}{5}$.

The negative reciprocal of -5 is $-\left(-\frac{1}{5}\right) = \frac{1}{5}$.

(3) The diagonals of a square are always perpendicular to each other.

Therefore, we have $PR \perp SQ$.

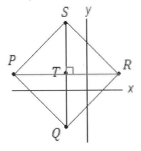

Since the slope of ST (which is the same as the slope of SQ) is $-5 = \frac{-5}{1}$, it follows that the slope of PR is $\frac{1}{5}$ (the negative reciprocal of $-5 = \frac{-5}{1}$).

(4) The figure is a bit deceptive here. It looks like PR is a horizontal line. This might lead someone to believe that the equation of the line is $y = 2$ (choice A). The figure is not drawn to scale however, and so we need to use the points given in the question, and not the figure to get the answer.

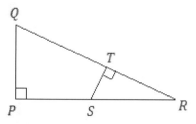

Note: Figure not drawn to scale.

108. In the right triangle PQR above, $SR = 9$, and $QR = 24$. If the length of $\overline{PR}$ is 2 units less than three times the length of $\overline{TR}$, what is the length of $\overline{PR}$?

   (A) $\frac{16}{21}$
   (B) $\frac{30}{7}$
   (C) 6
   (D) 16

* We redraw the two triangles next to each other so that congruent angles match up, and label the sides.

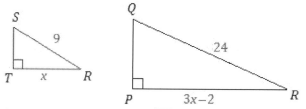

Note that if we let x be the length of $\overline{TR}$, then the length of $\overline{PR}$ is $3x - 2$. We now set up a ratio, cross multiply, and divide.

$$\frac{9}{24} = \frac{x}{3x - 2}$$
$$9(3x - 2) = 24x$$
$$27x - 18 = 24x$$
$$3x = 18$$

So $x = \frac{18}{3} = 6$, and it follows that the length of $\overline{PR}$ is $3x - 2 = 3 \cdot 6 - 2 = 18 - 2 = 16$, choice D.

Notes: (1) The two triangles are **similar**. This means that their angles are congruent.

122

(2) Similar triangles **do not** have to be the same size.

(3) To show that two triangles are similar we need only show that two pairs of angles are congruent. We get the third pair for free because all triangles have angle measures summing to 180 degrees.

In this problem both triangles share $\angle R$, and they each have a right angle ($\angle T$ and $\angle P$).

(4) **Corresponding sides of similar triangles are in proportion.**

So for example, in this problem, $\frac{SR}{QR} = \frac{TR}{PR}$.

(5) Once you find that $x = 6$, be careful to check again what the question is asking for. We are not being asked to find TR. We are being asked to find PR which is equal to $3x - 2$.

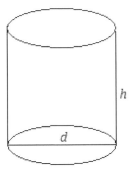

$$SA = 2\pi\left(\frac{d}{2}\right)^2 + \pi dh$$

109. The formula above can be used to calculate the total surface area of the right circular cylinder shown, where h is the height of the cylinder, and d is the diameter of each circular base. What must the expression πdh represent?

    (A) The area of a circular base
    (B) The sum of the areas of the two circular bases.
    (C) The lateral surface area
    (D) The sum of the area of one circular base and the lateral surface area.

Solution by process of elimination: The formula for the area of a circle is $A = \pi r^2$, where r is the radius of the circle (this formula is given at the beginning of each math section).

123

Recall that the diameter of a circle is twice the radius. That is, $d = 2r$. Solving this equation for r gives us $r = \frac{d}{2}$. So, in terms of d, the area of a circle is $A = \pi \left(\frac{d}{2}\right)^2$.

It follows that $2\pi \left(\frac{d}{2}\right)^2$ represents the sum of the areas of the two circular bases.

This leaves πdh as the lateral surface area, choice C.

* Direct solution: When we cut and unfold the cylinder we get the following rectangle.

Notice that the width of the rectangle is the circumference of the base of the cylinder.

The lateral surface area of the cylinder is the area of this rectangle.

$$L = Ch = 2\pi rh = \pi dh$$

So the answer is choice C.

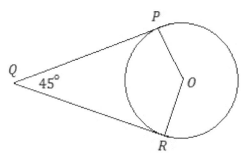

110. In the figure above, O is the center of the circle, line segments PQ and RQ are tangent to the circle at points P and R, respectively. The two segments intersect at point Q as shown. If the length of minor arc $\widehat{PR}$ is 9, what is the circumference of the circle?

124

* Since PQ is tangent to the circle and OP is a radius of the circle, we have $QP \perp OP$. Therefore $m\angle P = 90°$. Similarly, $m\angle R = 90°$. It follows that $m\angle O = 360 - 90 - 90 - 45 = 135°$. Since a central angle has the same measure as the arc it intercepts, minor arc $\overparen{PR}$ measures $135°$ as well. We can now find the circumference of the circle by setting up a ratio:

$$\frac{135}{360} = \frac{9}{C}$$

We cross multiply to get $135C = 3240$. Finally, we divide by 135 to get $C = \frac{3240}{135} = \mathbf{24}$.

Notes: (1) Notice that $\overline{OP}$ and $\overline{OR}$ are both radii of the circle. Therefore, $OP = OR$.

(2) A tangent line to a circle is always perpendicular to the appropriate radius of the circle.

In this problem $QP \perp OP$ and $QR \perp OR$. Therefore $m\angle P = m\angle R = 90°$.

(3) $OPQR$ is a quadrilateral. The angle measures of a quadrilateral sum to $360°$. It follows that $m\angle O + m\angle P + m\angle Q + m\angle R = 360°$.

(4) $\angle POR$ is a **central angle** of the circle because it's vertex is at the center of the circle.

The measure of a central angle is equal to the measure of the arc it intercepts.

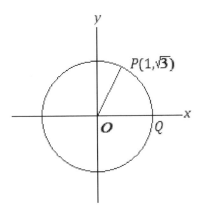

111. In the xy-plane above, O is the center of the circle, and the measure of $\angle POQ$ is $\frac{2\pi}{b}$ radians. What is the value of b ?

125

* Solution using a 30, 60, 90 triangle: We draw a right triangle inside the picture

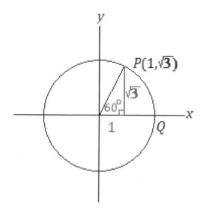

Observe that $\angle POQ$ measures $60°$. Converting to radians gives us

$$\frac{60\pi}{180} = \frac{\pi}{3} \text{ radians.}$$

So we have $\frac{2\pi}{b} = \frac{\pi}{3}$. Cross multiplying gives us $\pi b = 6\pi$, and so $b = $ **6**.

Notes: (1) If we had forgotten that the correct angle in that picture was $60°$, we could also use the TAN^{-1} button (2ND TAN) to get $\tan^{-1}\frac{\sqrt{3}}{1} = 60$.

Of course we can do this only if we are allowed to use a calculator for the problem.

Also, make sure your calculator is in degree mode when doing this computation.

(2) See problem 10 for more information on the special 30, 60, 90 triangle used here.

112. In triangles CAT and DOG, the measures of angles A and O are $90°$. Triangle DOG is similar to triangle CAT, with vertices D, O, and F corresponding to vertices C, A, and T, respectively. $CA = 24$, $CT = 26$, and each side of triangle DOG is $\frac{3}{7}$ the length of the corresponding side of triangle CAT. What is the value of $\tan G$?

* Let's draw a picture. We start by drawing the two triangles next to each other so that congruent angles match up, and label the side lengths that we were given.

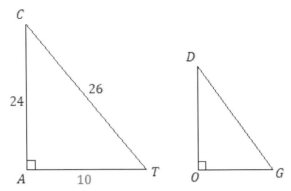

We can get AT by using the Pythagorean triple 5, 12, 13, and observing that $24 = 2 \cdot 12$, $26 = 2 \cdot 13$, and $10 = 2 \cdot 5$ (if you don't remember this Pythagorean triple, you can use the Pythagorean Theorem).

Now, $\tan G = \dfrac{\text{OPP}}{\text{ADJ}} = \dfrac{DO}{OG} = \dfrac{CA}{AT} = \dfrac{24}{10} = \mathbf{12/5}$ or $\mathbf{2.4}$.

Notes: (1) See problems 10 and 48 for more information on the Pythagorean Theorem and Pythagorean triples, respectively.

(2) See problems 12 and 108 for more information on the trigonometry needed here and similar triangles, respectively.

(3) The specific value $\dfrac{3}{7}$ is not important here. The only thing this number is needed for is to tell us that the two triangles are similar. Once we have that, we get $\dfrac{DO}{OG} = \dfrac{CA}{AT}$.

(4) Trigonometric functions behave the same on the corresponding angles of similar triangles. For example, $\tan G = \tan T = \dfrac{24}{10}$.

LEVEL 4: PASSPORT TO ADVANCED MATH

113. Which of the following is an equivalent form of the expression $(3x - 5)^2 + (3x - 5)$?

    (A) $3x - 5$
    (B) $9x^2 + 3x + 20$
    (C) $9x^2 - 27x - 5$
    (D) $(3x - 5)(3x - 4)$

Solution by recognizing a block: There is a block of $3x - 5$. So let's set $u = 3x - 5$. We then have

$$(3x - 5)^2 + (3x - 5) = u^2 + u = u(u + 1) = (3x - 5)(3x - 4)$$

This is choice D.

Notes: (1) We define a **block** to be an algebraic expression that appears more than once in a given problem. Very often in SAT problems a block can be treated just like a variable. In particular, blocks should usually not be manipulated—treat them as a single unit.

In this question, the block is $3x - 5$ because it appears twice.

(2) We substitute the block with a single variable to create an equivalent question that is easier to visualize.

(3) The expression $u^2 + u$ factors as $u(u + 1)$.

(4) If $u = 3x - 5$, then $u + 1 = (3x - 5) + 1 = 3x - 4$

(5) With a little practice you may not need to substitute the block for a single variable (see the next solution for details).

(6) This problem can also be solved by picking numbers. I leave this solution as an exercise for the reader.

* **Direct solution by factoring:** We can factor out $3x - 5$ from the expression to get $(3x - 5)(3x - 5 + 1) = (3x - 5)(3x - 4)$, choice D.

Solution by expanding:

$$(3x - 5)^2 = (3x - 5)(3x - 5) = 9x^2 - 30x + 25$$

So we have

$$(3x - 5)^2 + (3x - 5) = 9x^2 - 30x + 25 + 3x - 5 = 9x^2 - 27x + 20$$

At this point we can eliminate choices A, B, and C. So the answer is D.

Notes: (1) There are several ways to multiply two binomials. One way is by FOILing, and another method was shown in problem 53. Let's look at the second method in some detail.

$$
\begin{array}{r}
3x - 5 \\
\underline{3x - 5} \\
-15x + 25 \\
\underline{9x^2 - 15x + 0} \\
9x^2 - 30x + 25
\end{array}
$$

What we did here is mimic the procedure for ordinary multiplication. We begin by multiplying -5 by -5 to get 25. We then multiply -5 by $3x$ to get $-15x$. This is where the first row under the first line comes from.

Next we put 0 in as a placeholder on the next line. We then multiply $3x$ by -5 to get $-15x$. And then we multiply $3x$ by $3x$ to get $9x^2$. This is where the second row under the first line comes from.

Now we add the two rows to get $9x^2 - 30x + 25$.

114. A radioactive substance decays at an annual rate of 8 percent. If the initial amount of the substance is 800 grams, which of the following functions h models the remaining amount of the substance, in grams, t years later?

　　(A) $h(t) = 0.08(800)^t$
　　(B) $h(t) = 0.92(800)^t$
　　(C) $h(t) = 800(0.08)^t$
　　(D) $h(t) = 800(0.92)^t$

Solution using a general exponential function: Recall that a general exponential function has the form $P(t) = a \cdot (1 + r)^{ct}$, where $a = P(0)$ is the initial amount and r is the growth rate.

In this problem, $a = P(0) = 800$, and since the substance is decaying at an annual rate of 8 percent, $c = 1$, and the exponential rate is $r = -.08$. So we have $P(t) = 800(1 - .08)^t = 800(0.92)^t$, choice D.

Notes: (1) A general exponential function has the form $f(t) = a \cdot (1+r)^{ct}$, where $a = f(0)$ is the *initial amount* and r is the *growth rate*. If $r > 0$, then we have **exponential growth** and if $r < 0$ we have **exponential decay**.

In this problem, we are given that the substance *decays*, and so we must have $r < 0$. This is why $r = -0.08$, instead of 0.08.

(2) We have $c = 1$ because the growth rate is annual (once per year). In other words, after exactly 1 year 8 percent of the substance will be gone. After another year, 8 percent of what remains will be gone... and so on.

In general, c tells us how often that percentage of the substance disappears. For example, if the substance decays at a semiannual rate (twice per year, or once every 6 months), then $c = 2$.

x	$g(x)$
-3	1
0	2
3	0
6	-5

115. The function g is defined by a polynomial. Some values of x and $g(x)$ are shown in the table above. Which of the following must be a factor of $g(x)$?

(A) $x - 4$
(B) $x - 3$
(C) $x - 1$
(D) $x + 3$

* Solution using the factor theorem: According to the chart, we have $g(3) = 0$. By the factor theorem $x - 3$ is a factor of $g(x)$, choice B.

Notes: (1) Recall that a number r is a **root** (or **zero**, or **solution**) of a function g if $g(r) = 0$.

(2) The **factor theorem** says that r is a root of the polynomial $g(x)$ if and only if $x - r$ is a factor of the polynomial.

116. If $\sqrt[3]{k^4} \cdot \sqrt[7]{k^5} = k^m$ for all values of k, what is the value of m ?

(A) $\dfrac{20}{21}$

(B) $\dfrac{7}{4}$

(C) $\dfrac{43}{21}$

(D) $\dfrac{27}{4}$

* $\sqrt[3]{k^4} \cdot \sqrt[7]{k^5} = k^{\frac{4}{3}} \cdot k^{\frac{5}{7}} = k^{\frac{4}{3}+\frac{5}{7}} = k^{\frac{4\cdot7+3\cdot5}{3\cdot7}} = k^{\frac{28+15}{21}} = k^{\frac{43}{21}}.$

So $m = \dfrac{43}{21}$, choice C.

Notes: (1) For the laws of exponents used here, see the table in problem 72.

For example, we used the law $x^a x^b$ to get $k^{\frac{4}{3}} \cdot k^{\frac{5}{7}} = k^{\frac{4}{3}+\frac{5}{7}}$.

(2) We can rewrite the expression $\sqrt[c]{a^b}$ using only an exponent as $a^{\frac{b}{c}}$. In the expression $a^{\frac{b}{c}}$, a is the base, b is the power, and c is the root.

For example, $\sqrt[3]{k^4} = k^{\frac{4}{3}}$ and $\sqrt[7]{k^5} = k^{\frac{5}{7}}$.

(3) If we are allowed to use a calculator for this problem, then we can add $\dfrac{4}{3}$ and $\dfrac{5}{7}$ by typing the following into our TI-84 calculator:

$$4/3 + 5/7 \text{ ENTER MATH ENTER ENTER}$$

The output will be 43/21.

(4) If a calculator is not allowed, we can use the following:

$$\frac{a}{b} + \frac{c}{d} = \frac{ad+bc}{bd}$$

For example, $\dfrac{4}{3} + \dfrac{5}{7} = \dfrac{4\cdot7+3\cdot5}{3\cdot7} = \dfrac{28+15}{21} = \dfrac{43}{21}.$

117. If j and k are positive numbers such that $5j = 7k$, what is the value of $\dfrac{j+k}{k}$???

* **Solution by picking numbers:** We choose values for j and k that satisfy the given equation. The simplest choice is $j = 7$ and $k = 5$. It follows that

$$\frac{j+k}{k} = \frac{7+5}{5} = 12/5.$$

Note: We can also grid in the decimal 2.4.

Algebraic solution: First note that $\frac{j}{k} = \frac{7}{5}$. So we have

$$\frac{j+k}{k} = \frac{j}{k} + \frac{k}{k} = \frac{7}{5} + 1 = \frac{7}{5} + \frac{5}{5} = \frac{7+5}{5} = 12/5 \text{ or } 2.4.$$

Notes: (1) To find $\frac{j}{k}$, we can use **cross division**. We divide both sides of the equation $5j = 7k$ by $5k$ to get $\frac{j}{k} = \frac{7}{5}$.

(2) Most students have no trouble at all adding two fractions with the same denominator. For example,

$$\frac{j}{k} + \frac{k}{k} = \frac{j+k}{k}$$

But these same students have trouble reversing this process.

$$\frac{j+k}{k} = \frac{j}{k} + \frac{k}{k}$$

Note that these two equations are **identical** except that the left and right hand sides have been switched. Note also that to break a fraction into two (or more) pieces, the original denominator is repeated for **each** piece.

$$f(x) = \frac{1}{(x-3)^2 - 8(x-3) + 16}$$

118. For what value of x is the function f above undefined?

* f will be undefined when the denominator is zero. So we solve the equation $(x-3)^2 - 8(x-3) + 16 = 0$. The left hand side of the equation factors as $(x - 3 - 4)^2 = 0$, or equivalently $(x - 7)^2 = 0$. So $x - 7 = 0$, and therefore, $x = \mathbf{7}$.

Notes: (1) Many students might find it hard to see how to factor the expression $(x-3)^2 - 8(x-3) + 16$. To help see how to do this we can make a formal substitution of $u = x - 3$. The expression then becomes $u^2 - 8u + 16$ which factors as $(u-4)^2$. The equation $(u-4)^2 = 0$ has solution $u = 4$. But remember that $u = x - 3$. So we have $x - 3 = 4$, and so $x = 4 + 3 = 7$.

(2) In note (1), we are regarding $x - 3$ as a **block**. See problem 113 for more information on blocks.

$$h(x) = (x - 3)(x + 7)$$

119. If we rewrite the function h shown above in the form $h(x) = (x - a)^2 + b$, where a and b are real numbers, then what is the value of $a - b$?

*Quick solution The x-intercepts of the graph of this function (which is a parabola) are $(3, 0)$ and $(-7, 0)$. The x-coordinate of the vertex is midway between 3 and -7. So the vertex has x-coordinate $\frac{3-7}{2} = -2$.

The y-coordinate of the vertex is

$$h(-2) = (-2 - 3)(-2 + 7) = (-5)(5) = -25$$

So $a = -2$, $b = -25$, and $a - b = -2 - (-25) = -2 + 25 = \textbf{23}$.

Note: The standard form for a quadratic function is

$$y - k = a(x - h)^2.$$

The graph is a parabola with **vertex** at (h, k). The parabola opens upwards if $a > 0$ and downwards if $a < 0$.

For example, the graph of $h(x) = (x + 2)^2 - 25$ is an upward facing parabola with vertex $(-2, -25)$.

Algebraic solution (by completing the square): We first put the function h into general form by expanding the product

$$(x - 3)(x + 7) = x^2 + 4x - 21.$$

We now complete the square on $x^2 + 4x$ to get $x^2 + 4x + 4$.

So $x^2 + 4x - 21 = x^2 + 4x + 4 - 4 - 21 = (x + 2)^2 - 25$.

Thus, $a = -2$, $b = -25$, and $a - b = -2 - (-25) = -2 + 25 = \textbf{23}$.

Notes: (1) The **general form** for the equation of a parabola is

$$y = ax^2 + bx + c.$$

We can put the function $y = h(x)$ into general form by simply multiplying $(x - 3)$ and $(x + 7)$ together to get

$$(x - 3)(x + 7) = x^2 + 4x - 21.$$

This form however is not that useful for identifying specific information about the parabola such as the vertex.

(2) The **standard form** for the equation of a parabola is

$$y = a(x - h)^2 + k, \text{ or equivalently, } y - k = a(x - h)^2$$

In either of these forms, we can identify the vertex of the parabola as (h, k).

(3) To change an equation of a parabola from general form to standard form, we use a procedure called **completing the square**.

To complete the square on the expression $x^2 + bx$, we take half of the number b, and square the result to get b^2.

For example, to complete the square on $x^2 + 4x$, we take half of 4 to get 2, and then square 2 to get $2^2 = 4$.

We then add this to the original expression to get $x^2 + 4x + 4$. This new expression is a perfect square. In fact, it factors as follows:

$$x^2 + 4x + 4 = (x + 2)(x + 2) = (x + 2)^2$$

Note that the number 2 is the same as the number we got from taking half of 4. This is not a coincidence. It always happens.

(4) Completing the square *does not* produce an expression that is equivalent to the original expression. For example, the expression $(x + 2)^2 = x^2 + 4x + 4$ is 4 more than the original expression $x^2 + 4x$.

We can fix this problem by adding and subtracting what we need to the right hand side of the equation. We write $h(x) = x^2 + 4x + 4 - 4 - 21$.

Notice how we added and subtracted 4 between $4x$ and -21.

We can now simplify this expression to

$$h(x) = x^2 + 4x + 4 - 25 = (x + 2)^2 - 25$$

(5) Once the equation is in the standard form

$$h(x) = (x + 2)^2 - 25 \quad \text{or} \quad h(x) + 25 = (x + 2)^2$$

we can easily pick out the vertex by matching the equation up with the standard form

$$y = a(x - h)^2 + k \quad \text{or} \quad y - k = a(x - h)^2$$

Observe that $h = -2$ and $k = -25$.

(6) Try not to confuse the constant h used in the standard form with the function h (always written as $h(x)$ here) given in the problem. The function's name is an unfortunate choice here, as h is almost always used as the generic name for the x-intercept of the vertex of a parabola.

(7) It is very common for students to make sign errors here. Note that the expression $(x + 2)^2$ indicates that $h = -2$, and also the expression $h(x) + 25$ indicates that $k = -25$.

To see this, note that

$$(x + 2)^2 = \left(x - (-2)\right)^2 \quad \text{and} \quad h(x) + 25 = h(x) - (-25).$$

$$f(x) = x^2 - 9x + 6$$

120. Let a be the product of the roots of the function f shown above, and let b be the sum of the roots of f. What is the value of $\frac{a}{b}$?

* The product of the roots of f is $a = 6$ and the sum of the roots of f is $b = 9$. So $\frac{a}{b} = \frac{6}{9} = \mathbf{2/3}$.

Notes: (1) Let r and s be the roots of the quadratic equation
$$x^2 + bx + c = 0.$$
Then
$$b = -(r + s) \quad \text{and} \quad c = rs.$$
In other words, the constant term c is the product of the roots, and the coefficient of x, namely b, is the negative of the sum of the roots.

(2) We can also grid in one of the decimals $.\mathbf{666}$ or $.\mathbf{667}$.

LEVEL 4: PROBLEM SOLVING AND DATA

Questions 121 - 122 refer to the following information.

Data was collected on attendees to a theatre production over a period of six months. Each attendee was required to purchase a ticket for admission. The ticket prices for afternoon matinees and evening performances were the same, and the cost of tickets did not change during the six-month period.

	Attended an afternoon matinee	Attended an evening performance	Total tickets purchased	Total money earned from tickets ($)
Purchased orchestra seat	4,345	9,873	14,218	5,274,878
Purchased mezzanine seat	8,276	11,375	19,651	3,714,039
Purchased balcony seat	11,354	11,021	22,375	1,700,500
Total	23,975	32,269	56,244	10,689,417

121. * What was the total cost for three balcony seats?

    (A) $76
    (B) $228
    (C) $567
    (D) $1113

* The cost for one balcony seat was 1,700,500 / 22,375 = 76 dollars. It follows that the cost for three balcony seats was 3 · 76 = 228 dollars, choice B.

122. * Based on the table, what is the approximate probability that an attendee of an afternoon matinee purchased an orchestra seat?

    (A) 0.08
    (B) 0.18
    (C) 0.25
    (D) 0.30

136

* 23,975 people attended an afternoon matinee, and of these attendees 4,345 purchased an orchestra seat. It follows that the desired probability is $\frac{4,345}{23,975} \approx 0.18$. So the answer is choice B.

Notes: (1) The denominator of the fraction is 23,975, the total number of attendees of an afternoon matinee. To find this number we look in the column labeled "Attended an afternoon matinee" and the row labeled "Total."

(2) The numerator of the fraction is 4,345, the number of afternoon matinee attendees who purchased an orchestra seat. To find this number we look in the column labeled "Attended an afternoon matinee" and the row labeled "Purchased orchestra seat."

Technical Remarks: (1) In this question we are being asked to use the table to compute a **conditional probability**. Let's name the events as follows: M will stand for "the attendee attended an afternoon matinee," and O will stand for "the attendee purchased an orchestra seat."

(2) The requested probability is $P(O|M)$. This is read as "the probability that the attendee purchased an orchestra seat given that the attendee attended an afternoon matinee" (in particular, the vertical line is read "given"). We can say this more simply as "the probability that an attendee of an afternoon matinee purchased an orchestra seat."

123. The value of an emerald is expected to increase by 4 percent from one year to the next beginning in year 2017. What type of relationship should be expected between the age of the diamond and the diamond's value?

    (A) Linear relationship
    (B) Quadratic relationship
    (C) Cubic relationship
    (D) Exponential relationship

* **Direct solution:** The value of the emerald is modeled by $V = k(1.04)^t$, where k is the initial value of the emerald and t is the number of years after 2017. This is an exponential relationship, choice D.

Notes: (1) A linear relationship has the form $y = ax + b$

(2) A quadratic relationship has the form $y = ax^2 + bx + c$

(3) A cubic relationship has the form $y = ax^3 + bx^2 + cx + d$

(4) An exponential relationship has the form $y = a(1 + r)^{ct}$

(5) Let's suppose that the value of the emerald at the beginning of 2017 (the initial value) is k. There are two ways we can increase k by 4 percent.

Method 1: We can take 4% of k, and then add the result to k:

$$k + 0.04k = 1k + 0.04k = (1 + 0.04)k = 1.04k$$

Method 2: Note that increasing k by 4% is the same as taking 104% of k:

$$1.04k$$

See problem 89 for more information on these two methods.

So when $t = 1$, the value of the emerald will be $V = k(1.04)$.

(6) In Note (5) We saw that at the beginning of 2018 ($t = 1$), the value of the emerald will be $V = k(1.04)$. In another year, the value of the emerald will increase another 4%. Using Method 2 in Note (5), we see that we need to once again multiply by (1.04). When we do this, we get $V = k(1.04)(1.04) = k(1.04)^2$.

Notice that the number of years ($t = 2$) matches the exponent.

(7) Continuing as in Notes (5) and (6), we see that after t years, the value of the emerald is $V = k(1.04)^t$. This defines an exponential relationship where $a = k$, $r = 0.04$, and $c = 1$ (see Note (4)).

(8) A general exponential function has the form $f(t) = a(1 + r)^{ct}$, where $a = f(0)$ is the *initial amount* and r is the *growth rate*. If $r > 0$, then we have **exponential growth** and if $r < 0$ we have **exponential decay**.

In this problem we have exponential growth because $r = 0.04 > 0$.

124. If the average (arithmetic mean) of a, b, and 23 is 12, what is the average of a and b?

    (A) 6.5
    (B) 11
    (C) 13
    (D) It cannot be determined from the information given.

* **Solution by changing averages to sums:** The Sum of the 3 numbers is $12 \cdot 3 = 36$. Thus $a + b + 23 = 36$, and it follows that $a + b = 13$. So the Average of a and b is $\frac{13}{2} = 6.5$, choice A.

Notes: (1) A problem involving averages often becomes much easier when we first convert the averages to sums. We can easily change an average to a sum using the following simple formula: **Sum = Average · Number**

(2) In this problem we are given that the Average is 12.

Since we are averaging three numbers (a, b, and 23), the Number is 3.

Using the formula from note (1) we get that the Sum of a, b, and 23 is $12 \cdot 3 = 36$.

Solution by picking numbers: Let's let $a = 1$ and $b = 12$. We make this choice because 1 and 23 are both 11 units from 12. Then the Average of a and b is $\frac{a + b}{2} = \frac{1 + 12}{2} = \frac{13}{2} = 6.5$, choice A.

125. A square garden measures 8 feet by 8 feet. Eight biologists each mark off a randomly selected square region with side length 1 foot. There is no overlap between any of the regions. Each biologist counts the potato bugs contained in the soil to a depth of 1 foot beneath the surface in each region. The results are shown in the table below.

Region	Number of potato bugs	Region	Number of potato bugs
I	44	V	35
II	53	VI	72
III	51	VII	31
IV	60	VIII	62

Which of the following is a reasonable approximation of the number of potato bugs to a depth of 1 foot beneath the garden's surface in the entire garden?

(A)   50
(B)   400
(C)   3,200
(D) 25,600

* **Solution by estimation:** We add up all of the numbers in the table to get 408, which is approximately 400. So 8 square feet of the garden contains approximately 400 potato bugs to a depth of 1 foot beneath the garden's surface.

But the size of the garden is $8 \cdot 8 = 64$ square feet. So we need to multiply 400 by 8 to get $8 \cdot 400 = 3,200$, choice C.

Notes: (1) The average of the numbers seems to be somewhere near 50 (some numbers are a bit more than 50 and other numbers are a bit less than 50). It's okay if this estimate is off a bit because the answer choices are so far away from each other.

(2) Using note (1), we can get a quick estimate for the sum of the entries in the table by multiplying 50 by the number of entries 8. We get a sum of $8 \cdot 50 = 400$.

(3) Alternatively, we can use our calculator to actually add up all the numbers to get a more precise answer of 408.

(4) Whether we use 400 or 408, we are still just getting an estimate in the end. The 408 is just the number of potato bugs in 8 of the 64 square feet. We actually have no idea how many potato bugs are in the remaining 56 square feet. But $8 \cdot 400$ or $8 \cdot 408$ are both reasonable guesses for a rough estimate.

Questions 126 - 127 refer to the following information.

$$r = \sqrt{\frac{P}{4\pi I}}$$

Given that the power of the radio signal from a radio antenna is P, the distance from the radio antenna r is related to the intensity of the signal I by the formula above.

126. Which of the following expresses the intensity of the radio signal in terms of the distance from the radio antenna and the power of the signal?

(A) $I = \dfrac{Pr^2}{4\pi}$

(B) $I = \dfrac{4\pi P}{r^2}$

(C) $I = \dfrac{r^2}{4\pi P}$

(D) $I = \dfrac{P}{4\pi r^2}$

* **Algebraic solution:** We square each side of the given equation to get

$r^2 = \frac{P}{4\pi I}$. We then multiply each side of this last equation by $4\pi I$ to get $4\pi I r^2 = P$. Finally, we divide each side by $4\pi r^2$ to get $I = \frac{P}{4\pi r^2}$, choice D.

Note: Instead of multiplying each side of the equation $r^2 = \frac{P}{4\pi I}$ by $4\pi I$, we can just multiply by I, while simultaneously dividing each side of the equation by r^2 to get $I = \frac{P}{4\pi r^2}$ more quickly.

Solution by picking numbers: Let's let $P = \pi$ and $I = 1$. It follows that

$$r = \sqrt{\frac{\pi}{4\pi}} = \sqrt{\frac{1}{4}} = \frac{\sqrt{1}}{\sqrt{4}} = \frac{1}{2}.$$

Substituting $P = \pi$, $r = \frac{1}{2}$ and $I = 1$ into each answer choice yields false equations for choices A, B, and C. So the answer must be D.

127. John and Grace are measuring the intensity of a radio signal coming from the same antenna. Grace is three times as far from the antenna as John. Grace's measurement is what fraction of John's measurement?

(A) $\frac{1}{3}$

(B) $\frac{1}{9}$

(C) $\frac{1}{54}$

(D) $\frac{1}{81}$

Solution by picking numbers: Let's let the power be $P = 1$, so that we have $I = \frac{P}{4\pi r^2} = \frac{1}{4\pi r^2}$ (from the solution to the last problem). Let's let John's distance be 1 and Grace's distance be 3. Then for John, the intensity is $I = \frac{1}{4\pi \cdot 1^2} = \frac{1}{4\pi}$, and for Grace, the intensity is $I = \frac{1}{4\pi \cdot 3^2} = \frac{1}{36\pi}$.

Finally, we have $\frac{1}{36\pi} \div \frac{1}{4\pi} = \frac{1}{36\pi} \cdot \frac{4\pi}{1} = \frac{1}{9}$, choice B.

* **Direct solution:** If John's distance is r, then Grace's distance is $3r$, and we have $\frac{P}{4\pi(3r)^2} \div \frac{P}{4\pi r^2} = \frac{P}{4\pi \cdot 9r^2} \cdot \frac{4\pi r^2}{P} = \frac{1}{9}$, choice B.

141

128. A survey was taken of the gross income of families in a small town. It was found that the median gross income was $55,000 and the mean gross income was $82,000. Which of the following situations could explain the difference between the median and the mean gross income of families in the town?

(A) There are a few families that make much less income than the rest.
(B) There are a few families that make much more income than the rest.
(C) All of the families in the town have gross incomes that are close to each other.
(D) Many of the families make between $55,000 and $82,000.

* Direct solution: Since the median and mean are not equal, the data is not symmetrical. In particular, the mean is greater than the median. This means that there are large outliers in the data. In other words, there are a few families that make much more income than the rest, choice B.

Notes: (1) A distribution is **symmetrical** when the mean and median of the data are equal. A normal distribution is an example of a symmetrical distribution.

(2) In this problem the mean and median are not equal, and so it follows that the distribution is NOT symmetrical.

(3) A distribution that is not symmetrical contains **outliers**. These are a small group of data that are significantly larger or smaller than the rest of the data.

(4) If the outliers are larger than the rest of the data, then the mean will be greater than the median, and conversely. If the outliers are smaller than the rest of the data, then the mean will be less than the median, and conversely.

In this problem, the mean is greater than the median, and so the outliers are larger than the rest of the data.

Solution by picking numbers and changing averages to sums: To simplify things, let's use the numbers 55 and 82 for the median and mean, respectively.

142

Let's use three data points. We will make two of the data points 50 and 55, and choose the third so that the mean is 82.

Let's let our data points be 50, 55, and x. We use the formula

$$\text{Sum} = \text{Average} \cdot \text{Number}$$

To get that the sum of the three data points is $82 \cdot 3 = 246$.

So we have

$$50 + 55 + x = 246$$
$$105 + x = 246$$
$$x = 246 - 105 = 141$$

So the three data points are 50, 55, and 141.

Note that in this example there is one data point that is significantly greater than the rest. To be safe, let's check if each answer choice is true or false.

(A) False
(B) True
(C) False
(D) False

So the answer is choice B.

LEVEL 5: HEART OF ALGEBRA

129. If $t^{-2} - 4t^{-1} - 12 = 0$, which of the following could be the value of t ?

A. -6
B. -2
C. $-\dfrac{1}{2}$
D. $-\dfrac{1}{6}$

Solution using a substitution: We make the substitution $u = t^{-1}$. It follows that $u^2 = (t^{-1})^2 = t^{-2}$. So the given equation becomes

$$u^2 - 4u - 12 = 0.$$

We can solve this equation in several different ways. The quickest way in this case is by factoring.

$$(u - 6)(u + 2) = 0$$

$$u - 6 = 0 \quad \text{or} \quad u + 2 = 0$$

$$u = 6 \quad \text{or} \quad u = -2$$

We now replace u by t^{-1} and solve for t.

$$t^{-1} = 6 \quad \text{or} \quad t^{-1} = -2$$

$$t = \frac{1}{6} \quad \text{or} \quad t = -\frac{1}{2}$$

So the answer is C.

Notes: (1) We can solve the quadratic equation $u^2 - 4u - 12 = 0$ in several other ways. Here are two other methods:

Quadratic formula: We identify $a = 1$, $b = -4$, and $c = -12$.

$$u = \frac{-b \pm \sqrt{b^2 - 4ac}}{2a} = \frac{4 \pm \sqrt{16 + 48}}{2} = \frac{4 \pm \sqrt{64}}{2} = \frac{4 \pm 8}{2} = 2 \pm 4.$$

So we get $u = 2 + 4 = 6$ or $u = 2 - 4 = -2$.

Completing the square: For this solution we move the constant to the right hand side to get $u^2 - 4u = 12$.

We take half of -4, which is -2, and square this number to get 4. We then add 4 to each side of the equation to get $u^2 - 4u + 4 = 12 + 4$. This is equivalent to $(u - 2)^2 = 16$. We now apply the square root property to get $u - 2 = \pm 4$. So $u = 2 \pm 4$. This yields the solutions $2 + 4 = 6$, and $2 - 4 = -2$.

(2) Once we find u, we need to remember to replace u by t^{-1}.

(3) Recall that $t^{-1} = \frac{1}{t^1} = \frac{1}{t}$. So we can solve the equation $t^{-1} = 6$ by taking the reciprocal of each side of this equation. We get $t = \frac{1}{6}$.

Similarly, the equation $t^{-1} = -2$ has solution $t = \frac{1}{-2} = -\frac{1}{2}$.

* Solution without a formal substitution: We can factor the left hand side of the given equation as $t^{-2} - 4t^{-1} - 12 = (t^{-1} - 6)(t^{-1} + 2)$.

We set each factor equal to 0 to get $t^{-1} - 6 = 0$ or $t^{-1} + 2 = 0$.

So $t^{-1} = 6$ or $t^{-1} = -2$. Therefore, $t = \frac{1}{6}$ or $t = -\frac{1}{2}$.

The answer is C.

130. If $2a - 12b = 7$, what is the value of $\frac{5^a}{25^{3b}}$?

(A) 5^7

(B) $\sqrt{5^7}$

(C) 25^3

(D) The value cannot be determined from the information given.

* Algebraic solution: $\frac{5^a}{25^{3b}} = \frac{5^a}{(5^2)^{3b}} = \frac{5^a}{5^{6b}} = 5^{a-6b} = 5^{\frac{2a-12b}{2}} = 5^{\frac{7}{2}} = \sqrt{5^7}$.

This is choice B.

Notes: (1) See problem 72 for the laws of exponents used here.

(2) $\frac{2a-12b}{2} = \frac{2(a-6b)}{2} = a - 6b$.

131. A girl scout has k boxes, each containing 10 cookies. After visiting p parents and selling c cookies to each of them, she has d cookies remaining. Which of the following expresses p in terms of k, c, and d ?

A. $\dfrac{10k-d}{c}$

B. $\dfrac{10k+d}{c}$

C. $\dfrac{10k}{c} - d$

D. $\dfrac{10c-d}{k}$

Solution by picking numbers: Let's let $k = 2$, $p = 3$, and $c = 4$. So the girl scout has $2 \cdot 10 = 20$ cookies. She sells 4 cookies to each of 3 parents for a total of $4 \cdot 3 = 12$ cookies. It follows that she has $20 - 12 = 8$ left. So $d = 8$.

Since we are trying to find p, we put a nice big, dark circle around $p = 3$. We now check each answer choice.

A. $\dfrac{10k-d}{c} = \dfrac{20-8}{4} = \dfrac{12}{4} = 3$

B. $\dfrac{10k+d}{c} = \dfrac{20+8}{4} = \dfrac{28}{4} = 7$

C. $\dfrac{10k}{c} - d = \dfrac{20}{4} - 8 = 5 - 8 = -3$

D. $\dfrac{10c-d}{k} = \dfrac{40-8}{2} = \dfrac{32}{2} = 16$

Since choices B, C, and D came out incorrect we can eliminate them. So the answer is choice A.

* Algebraic solution: The girl scout has a total of $k \cdot 10 = 10k$ cookies (k boxes with 10 cookies per box). She sells a total of pc cookies (p parents and c cookies per parent). So the number of cookies she has remaining is $d = 10k - pc$.

We need to solve this last equation for p. We subtract $10k$ from each side of the equation to get $d - 10k = -pc$. We now divide each side of this last equation by $-c$ to get $p = \dfrac{d-10k}{-c} = \dfrac{-(d-10k)}{c} = \dfrac{10k-d}{c}$, choice A.

Note: To avoid all of the minus signs, we can also solve the equation $d = 10k - pc$ by adding pc to each side of the equation while simultaneously subtracting d from each side of the equation to get $pc = 10k - d$. We then just divide by c to get $p = \dfrac{10k-d}{c}$.

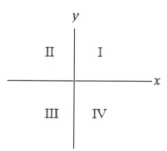

132. If the system of inequalities $y < 4x + 1$ and $y \geq -\dfrac{1}{2}x - 2$ is graphed in the xy-plane above, which quadrant contains no solutions to the system?

   (A) Quadrant I
   (B) Quadrant II
   (C) Quadrant III
   (D) There are solutions in all four quadrants.

* Complete algebraic solution: Let's sketch each inequality, one at a time, starting with $y < 4x + 1$. We first sketch the line $y = 4x + 1$ by plotting the two intercepts. We get the y-intercept by setting $x = 0$. In this case we get $y = 4 \cdot 0 + 1 = 1$. So the point $(0, 1)$ is on the line. We get the x-intercept by setting $y = 0$. In this case we get $0 = 4x + 1$, so that $-1 = 4x$, and $x = -\frac{1}{4}$. So the point $(-\frac{1}{4}, 0)$ is on the line. This line is shown in the figure on the left below. Note that we draw a dotted line because the strict inequality $<$ tells us that points on this line are not actually solutions to the inequality $y < 4x + 1$.

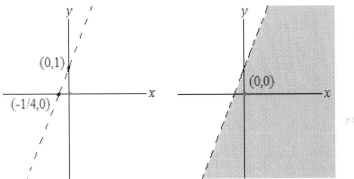

Now we need to figure out which direction to shade. To do this we plug any point *not on the line* into the inequality. For example, we can use $(0, 0)$. Substituting this point into $y < 4x + 1$ gives $0 < 1$. Since this expression is true, we shade the region that includes $(0, 0)$ as shown above in the figure on the right.

We now do the same thing for the second inequality. The intercepts of $y = -\frac{1}{2}x - 2$ are $(0, -2)$ and $(-4, 0)$. When we test $(0, 0)$ we get the true statement $0 \geq -2$.

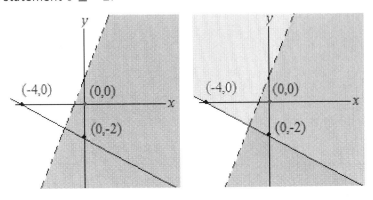

The figure on the above left shows the graph of $y = -\frac{1}{2}x - 2$ with the intercepts plotted, and the graph on the right shows three different shadings. The rightmost shading is the solution set of the given system.

Note that there are solutions in all four quadrants, choice D.

$$3x + 9y = 11$$
$$cx + dy = 55$$

133. In the system of equations above, c and d are constants. If the system has infinitely many solutions, what is the value of $\frac{c}{d}$?

The system of equations

$$3x + 9y = 11$$
$$cx + dy = 55$$

has infinitely many solutions if $\frac{3}{c} = \frac{9}{d} = \frac{11}{55}$. In particular, we must have $\frac{3}{c} = \frac{9}{d}$, or equivalently $\frac{c}{d} = \frac{3}{9} = 1/3$ or $.333$.

Notes: (1) In this problem we did not need to find c and d themselves.

(2) If we did need to find c we could solve the equation $\frac{3}{c} = \frac{11}{55}$ to get $11c = 3 \cdot 55$, and so $c = \frac{3 \cdot 55}{11} = 3 \cdot 5 = 15$.

(3) Similarly we can find d by solving $\frac{9}{d} = \frac{11}{55}$ to get $11d = 9 \cdot 55$, and so $d = \frac{9 \cdot 55}{11} = 9 \cdot 5 = 45$.

The **general form of an equation of a line** is $ax + by = c$ where a, b and c are real numbers. If $b \neq 0$, then the slope of this line is $m = -\frac{a}{b}$. If $b = 0$, then the line is vertical and has no slope.

Let us consider 2 such equations.

$$ax + by = c$$
$$dx + ey = f$$

(1) If there is a number r such that $ra = d$, $rb = e$, and $rc = f$, then the two equations represent the **same line**. Equivalently, the two equations represent the same line if $\frac{a}{d} = \frac{b}{e} = \frac{c}{f}$. In this case the system of equations has **infinitely many solutions**.

(2) If there is a number r such that $ra = d$, $rb = e$, but $rc \neq f$, then the two equations represent **parallel** but distinct lines. Equivalently, the two equations represent parallel but distinct lines if $\frac{a}{d} = \frac{b}{e} \neq \frac{c}{f}$. In this case the system of equations has **no solution**.

(3) Otherwise the two lines intersect in a single point. In this case $\frac{a}{d} \neq \frac{b}{e}$, and the system of equations has a **unique solution**.

These three cases are illustrated in the figure below.

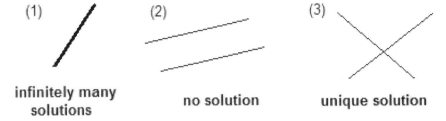

(1) infinitely many solutions

(2) no solution

(3) unique solution

Example: The following two equations represent the same line.

$$2x + 8y = 6$$
$$3x + 12y = 9$$

To see this note that $\frac{2}{3} = \frac{8}{12} = \frac{6}{9}$.(or equivalently, let $r = \frac{3}{2}$ and note that $\left(\frac{3}{2}\right)(2) = 3$, $\left(\frac{3}{2}\right)(8) = 12$, and $\left(\frac{3}{2}\right)(6) = 9$).

The following two equations represent parallel but distinct lines.

$$2x + 8y = 6$$
$$3x + 12y = 10$$

This time $\frac{2}{3} = \frac{8}{12} \neq \frac{6}{10}$.

The following two equations represent a pair of intersecting lines.

$$2x + 8y = 6$$
$$3x + 10y = 9$$

This time $\frac{2}{3} \neq \frac{8}{10}$.

134. On the number line, the distance between b and 1 is 5. What is the largest possible value for the distance between b and 3 on the number line?

* "The distance between b and 1 is 5" can be expressed mathematically as $|b - 1| = 5$. This equation is equivalent to the following two equations without absolute values.

$$b - 1 = -5 \quad \text{or} \quad b - 1 = 5$$

The solution to the first equation is $b = -5 + 1 = -4$, and the solution to the second equation is $b = 5 + 1 = 6$.

So b can be either -4 or 6. The distance between -4 and 3 is

$$|-4 - 3| = |-7| = 7.$$

The distance between 6 and 3 is

$$|6 - 3| = |3| = 3.$$

Since 7 is the larger of the two possible values, we grid in **7**.

Note: See problem 86 for a quick lesson in absolute value and distance.

135. * If $5x = 1 + 4y$ and $6x = 2 - 3y$, what is the value of x?

* **Solution using the elimination method:** Since we are trying to find x, we want to make y go away. So we make the two coefficients of y "match up" by multiplying by the appropriate numbers. We will multiply the first equation by 3 and the second equation by 4.

$$3(5x) = (1 + 4y)3$$
$$4(6x) = (2 - 3y)4$$

We distribute on the right hand side of each equation, and then add the two equations.

$$\begin{aligned} 15x &= 3 + 12y \\ \underline{24x} &= \underline{8 - 12y} \\ 39x &= 11 \end{aligned}$$

Now divide each side by 39 to get $x = \frac{11}{39}$. If we divide 11 by 39 in our calculator we get approximately $.28205128$. So we grid in $.\mathbf{282}$.

150

Note: See problem 70 for more information about the elimination method.

136. * The ionosphere is the layer of the earth's atmosphere that contains a high concentration of ions and free electrons and is able to reflect radio waves. It lies between about 40 to 620 miles above the Earth's surface. At a distance of 40 miles above the Earth's surface, the temperature is $-100°$ Fahrenheit, and at a distance of 600 miles above the Earth's surface, the temperature is $440°$ Fahrenheit. For every additional 40 miles from the Earth's surface, the temperature in the ionosphere increases by $T°$ Fahrenheit, where T is a constant. What is the value of T, to the nearest tenth?

* **Solution using slope:** We are given that the relationship between the distance above Earth's surface and temperature is linear.

If we think of distance as the independent variable and temperature as the dependent variable, then we see that the line contains the points $(40, -100)$ and $(600, 440)$. The slope of this line is

$$\frac{440 - (-100)}{600 - 40} = \frac{440 + 100}{560} = \frac{540}{560} \approx 0.9642857$$

This gives us the temperature increase for each additional mile. Since we want the temperature increase for each additional 40 miles, we need to multiply our last answer by 40 to get approximately 38.571428. To the nearest tenth, this is **38.6**.

Note: To avoid accidental error due to rounding too soon, it is best to use the answer in your calculator when multiplying by 40. For example, if we were to first round 0.9642857 to 0.96, and then multiply by 40, we would get the incorrect answer 38.4.

LEVEL 5: GEOMETRY AND TRIG

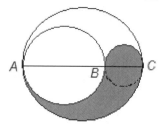

Note: Figure not drawn to scale

137. $\overline{AB}, \overline{BC}$, and $\overline{AC}$ are diameters of the three circles shown above. If $AC = 24$ and $AB = 5BC$, what is the area of the shaded region?

    (A) 48π
    (B) 24π
    (C) 12π
    (D) 6π

* We first find the diameter of each of the three circles.

Since $AC = AB + BC$, we have $24 = 5BC + BC = 6BC$. So $BC = \frac{24}{6} = 4$ and $AB = 5BC = 5 \cdot 4 = 20$.

Now we find the radius of each of the three circles by dividing their diameters by 2. The radius of the small circle is $\frac{4}{2} = 2$, the radius of the medium-sized circle is $\frac{20}{2} = 10$, and the radius of the largest circle is $\frac{24}{2} = 12$.

We can now find the area of the shaded region as follows.

$$A = \frac{1}{2}(\text{Area of big circle}) - \frac{1}{2}(\text{Area of medium circle}) + \frac{1}{2}(\text{Area of small circle})$$
$$= \frac{1}{2}(\pi \cdot 12^2) - \frac{1}{2}(\pi \cdot 10^2) + \frac{1}{2}(\pi \cdot 2^2)$$
$$= \frac{1}{2}(\pi \cdot 144) - \frac{1}{2}(\pi \cdot 100) + \frac{1}{2}(\pi \cdot 4)$$
$$= \frac{1}{2} \cdot 48\pi$$
$$= 24\pi$$

Thus, the answer is choice B.

138. A right circular cylinder has a base diameter of 4 and height 7. If point O is the center of the top of the cylinder and B lies on the circumference of the bottom of the cylinder, what is the straight-line distance between O and B ?

   (A) 3
   (B) 7
   (C) 11
   (D) $\sqrt{53}$

* **Solution:** We draw a right circular cylinder with a right triangle inside as follows.

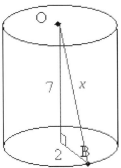

Note that the bottom leg of the triangle is equal to the radius of the circle (not the diameter) which is why it is 2 and not 4. We can now use the Pythagorean Theorem to find x.

$$x^2 = 2^2 + 7^2 = 4 + 49 = 53$$

So $x = \sqrt{53}$, choice D.

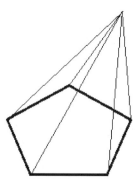

139. The figure above is a pyramid with four isosceles triangular faces and a base that is a regular pentagon. Points A, B, C, D and E (not shown) are the midpoints of the edges that are not in the plane of the base. Line segments are to be drawn on the triangular faces such that each segment connects two of these points. Which of the following is a representation of how these line segments could appear if viewed through the pentagonal base?

(A)   (B)

(C)   (D)

* The following picture illustrates the solution.

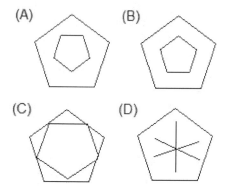

We have plotted points at the midpoint of each edge not in the plane of the base, then attached them with line segments drawn on the triangular faces. Finally, we lightly sketched the projection of the resulting pentagon onto the base. We see that the answer is choice B.

140. A ladder rests against the side of a wall and reaches a point that is 25 meters above the ground. The angle formed by the ladder and the ground is 58°. A point on the ladder is 3 meters from the wall. What is the vertical distance, in meters, from this point on the ladder to the ground?

(A) $22 \cos 58°$
(B) $25 - 3 \sin 58°$
(C) $25 - 3 \cos 58°$
(D) $25 - 3 \tan 58°$

* Let's draw a picture.

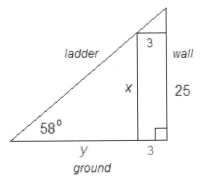

Note that there are two triangles in this picture. We will need to use both of them.

Also recall that for any angle A, $\tan A = \frac{\text{OPP}}{\text{ADJ}}$ (see problem 12). Using the smaller triangle we have $\tan 58° = \frac{x}{y}$, and using the larger triangle we have $\tan 58° = \frac{25}{y+3}$. The first equation gives $y \tan 58° = x$. and the second equation gives $(y + 3) \tan 58° = 25$. Distributing this last equation on the left gives $y \tan 58° + 3 \tan 58° = 25$. Substituting from the first equation yields $x + 3 \tan 58° = 25$. We subtract $3 \tan 58°$ from each side of this last equation to get $x = 25 - 3 \tan 58°$, choice D.

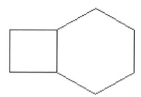

141. The figure above shows a regular hexagon and a square sharing a common side. If the area of the hexagon is $\frac{75\sqrt{3}}{2}$ square centimeters, what is the perimeter, in square centimeters, of the square?

* Recall that the hexagon consists of 6 equilateral triangles each of equal area.

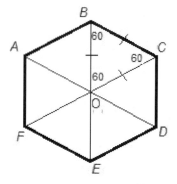

So the area of one of these triangles is $\frac{1}{6} \cdot \frac{75\sqrt{3}}{2} = \frac{25\sqrt{3}}{4}$. The side length of one of these triangles is then 5 (see notes below). Since the square and hexagon share a common side, the length of a side of the square is also 5. It follows that the perimeter of the square is $4 \cdot 5 = \mathbf{20}$.

Notes: (1) The area of an equilateral triangle with side length s is $A = \frac{\sqrt{3}}{4}s^2$ (see note (2) below).

In this problem we found that the area of one equilateral triangle was $\frac{25\sqrt{3}}{4}$. It follows that $\frac{\sqrt{3}}{4}s^2 = \frac{\sqrt{3}}{4} \cdot 25$. So $s^2 = 25$, and therefore, $s = 5$.

(2) Most students do not know the formula for the area of an equilateral triangle, so here is a quick derivation.

Let's start by drawing a picture of an equilateral triangle with side length s, and draw an **altitude** from a vertex to the opposite base. Note that an altitude of an equilateral triangle is the same as the **median** and **angle bisector** (this is in fact true for any isosceles triangle – see problem 144).

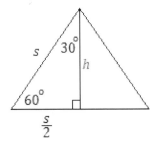

So we get two 30, 60, 90 right triangles with a leg of length $\frac{s}{2}$ and hypotenuse of length s.

We can find h by recalling that the side opposite the 60 degree angle has length $\sqrt{3}$ times the length of the side opposite the 30 degree angle. So $h = \frac{\sqrt{3}s}{2}$.

Alternatively, we can use the Pythagorean Theorem to find h:

$$h^2 = s^2 - \left(\frac{s}{2}\right)^2 = s^2 - \frac{s^2}{4} = \frac{3s^2}{4}. \text{ So } h = \frac{\sqrt{3}s}{2}.$$

It follows that the area of the triangle is

$$A = \frac{1}{2}\left(\frac{s}{2} + \frac{s}{2}\right)\left(\frac{\sqrt{3}s}{2}\right) = \frac{1}{2}s\left(\frac{\sqrt{3}s}{2}\right) = \frac{\sqrt{3}}{4}s^2.$$

142. A rectangular prism has a length that is 4 centimeters less than its height, and a width that is 4 centimeters more than its height. If the volume of the prism is 120 cubic centimeters, what is the surface area of the prism, in square centimeters?

* **Solution by guessing:** Let's guess that the height of the prism is 5 centimeters. It follows that the length is $5 - 4 = 1$ centimeter, and the width is $5 + 4 = 9$ centimeters. So the volume is $1 \cdot 9 \cdot 5 = 45$ cubic centimeters. This is too small.

Let's next guess that the height is 6 centimeters. It follows that the length is $6 - 4 = 2$ centimeters, and the width is $6 + 4 = 10$ centimeters. So the volume is $2 \cdot 10 \cdot 6 = 120$ cubic centimeters. This is correct.

The surface area, in square centimeters is

$$2 \cdot 2 \cdot 10 + 2 \cdot 2 \cdot 6 + 2 \cdot 10 \cdot 6 = 40 + 24 + 120 = \mathbf{184}.$$

Notes: (1) The **volume** of a rectangular prism is

$$V = lwh$$

where l, w and h are the length, width and height of the rectangular solid, respectively.

(2) The **surface area of a rectangular solid** is just the sum of the areas of all 6 faces. The formula is

$$A = 2lw + 2lh + 2wh$$

where l, w and h are the length, width and height of the rectangular solid, respectively.

Algebraic solution: If we let h be the height of the prism, in centimeters, then the length of the prism is $h - 4$ and the width of the prism is $h + 4$. It follows that the volume of the prism is $V = h(h - 4)(h + 4)$.

Since we are given that the volume of the prism is 120 cubic centimeters, we have $h(h - 4)(h + 4) = 120$.

There are several ways we can solve this equation for h.

Method 1 (Guessing): We take guesses for h as in the previous solution.

Method 2 (Graphically – if a calculator is allowed):

Press Y=   under Y_1 type X(X-4)(X+4)   under Y_2 type 120

Press WINDOW and set Ymax to a number greater than 120 (like 150, for example).

Press GRAPH, then CALC (2ND TRACE), select intersect, and press ENTER three times.

We get the solution X = 6.

So the height is 6 centimeters. It follows that the length is $6 - 4 = 2$ centimeters, and the width is $6 + 4 = 10$ centimeters. So the surface area, in square centimeters is

$$2 \cdot 2 \cdot 10 + 2 \cdot 2 \cdot 6 + 2 \cdot 10 \cdot 6 = 40 + 24 + 120 = \mathbf{184}.$$

143. In $\triangle ABC$, the length of side $\overline{BC}$ is 16 and the length of side $\overline{AC}$ is 17. What is the least possible integer length of side $\overline{AB}$?

* Solution using the triangle rule: By the triangle rule, we have that

$$17 - 16 < AB < 17 + 16.$$

That is, $1 < AB < 33$. Therefore, the least possible integer length of side AB is **2**.

Note: The triangle rule states that the length of the third side of a triangle is between the sum and difference of the lengths of the other two sides.

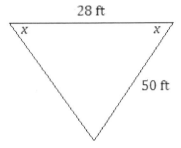

Note: Figure not drawn to scale.

144. * An architect drew a sketch of a triangular plot of land as shown above. Although the sketch was not drawn accurately to scale, the triangle was labeled with the proper dimensions. What is the value of $\tan x$?

* Since two of the angles of the triangle have equal measure, the triangle is isosceles. It follows that the median and altitude from the vertex of the triangle are the same.

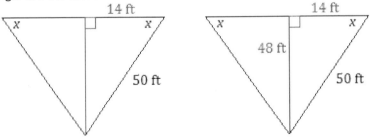

In the figure on the left we drew the altitude from the vertex angle. Since this is also the median, we get a right triangle with leg $\frac{28}{2} = 14$ ft. long.

We can now find the length of the other leg by using the Pythagorean Theorem, or better yet, by noticing that we have a multiple of the Pythagorean triple 7, 24, 25. Since $14 = 7 \cdot 2$ and $50 = 25 \cdot 2$, it follows that the length of the other leg is $24 \cdot 2 = 48$ ft.

Finally, we have $\tan x = \dfrac{\text{OPP}}{\text{ADJ}} = \dfrac{48}{14} = \mathbf{24/7}, \mathbf{3.42}$ or $\mathbf{3.43}$.

Notes: (1) A triangle is **isosceles** if it has two sides of equal length. Equivalently, an isosceles triangle has two angles of equal measure.

(2) An **altitude** of a triangle is perpendicular to the base. A **median** of a triangle splits the base into two equal parts. An **angle bisector** of a triangle splits an angle into two equal parts. In an isosceles triangle, the altitude, median, and angle bisector are all equal (when you choose the base that is **not** one of the equal sides).

(3) (1) See problems 10 and 48 for more information on the Pythagorean Theorem and Pythagorean triples, respectively.

LEVEL 5: PASSPORT TO ADVANCED MATH

145. For a polynomial $p(x)$, the value of $p(5)$ is -3. Which of the following must be true about $p(x)$?

    (A) $x - 8$ is a factor of $p(x)$.
    (B) $x - 3$ is a factor of $p(x)$.
    (C) $x + 3$ is a factor of $p(x)$.
    (D) The remainder when $p(x)$ is divided by $x - 5$ is -3.

* **Solution using the remainder theorem:** Since $p(5) = -3$, by the remainder theorem, the remainder when $p(x)$ is divided by $x - 5$ is -3, choice D.

Note: The **remainder theorem** says that $p(r) = a$ if and only if the remainder when $p(x)$ is divided by $x - r$ is a.

In this problem, $r = 5$ and $a = -3$.

Solution by picking a polynomial: If we let $p(x) = x^2 - 28$, then we have $p(5) = 5^2 - 28 = 25 - 28 = -3$. Since $x - 8$, $x - 3$, and $x + 3$ are not factors of this polynomial, we can eliminate choices A, B, and C. Therefore, the answer is choice D.

Notes: (1) $p(x) = x^2 - 28$ is a second-degree polynomial (or quadratic polynomial). It has *at most* two linear factors. It should be clear that $x - 8$, $x - 3$, and $x + 3$ cannot be factors of this polynomial. In fact, the two linear factors of this polynomial are $x - \sqrt{28}$ and $x + \sqrt{28}$.

(2) It might seem more reasonable to pick a linear polynomial instead of a quadratic one. In this case, the only linear polynomial satisfying the given condition is $p(x) = x - 8$ (Indeed, $p(5) = 5 - 8 = -3$). Although we can eliminate choices B and C using this polynomial, we cannot eliminate choice A. If you actually divide $x - 8$ by $x - 5$ (using either long division or synthetic division) you will see that the result is -3. So we cannot eliminate choice D either.

This is why I chose to use a quadratic polynomial instead of a linear one.

(3) We can actually use the constant function $p(x) = -3$. This is a polynomial of degree zero, and the given condition is trivially satisfied. Clearly this polynomial has no linear factors, and so we can eliminate choices A, B, and C.

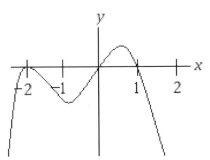

146. Which of the following could be an equation for the graph shown in the xy-plane above?

    (A) $y = x(x + 2)(1 - x)$
    (B) $y = x^2(x + 2)(x - 1)$
    (C) $y = x(x + 2)^2(1 - x)$
    (D) $y = x^2(x + 2)^3(x - 1)^2$

Solution by process of elimination: The answer choices show us that the answer must be a polynomial.

Since there are 3 turning points, the polynomial must have degree at least 4. We can therefore eliminate choice A (this polynomial has degree 3).

Since both "ends" of the graph go in the same direction (they both tend to $-\infty$), the polynomial must have even degree. This eliminates choice D (this polynomial has degree 7). Note that we can also use this same reasoning to eliminate choice A.

We can eliminate choice B by observing that if we plug a very large value of x into $y = x^2(x + 2)(x - 1)$, we will get a large positive value for y. But according to the graph we should get a negative value for y (since the graph is below the x-axis for large x).

So the answer is choice C.

Notes: (1) A **polynomial** has the form $a_n x^n + a_{n-1} x^{n-1} + \cdots + a_1 x + a_0$ where $a_0, a_1, ..., a_n$ are real numbers. For example, $x^2 + 2x - 35$ is a polynomial.

The degree of the polynomial is n. In other words, it is the highest power that appears in the expanded form of the polynomial.

(2) If a polynomial is in factored form, then we can get the degree of the polynomial by adding the degrees of the factors.

For example, the polynomial in choice A has degree $1 + 1 + 1 = 3$.

Similarly, the polynomials in choices B, C and D have degrees 4, 4 and 7, respectively.

(3) The "end behavior" of the graph of a polynomial can tell you whether the polynomial has even or odd degree. If both ends of the graph head in the same direction (both up to ∞, or both down to $-\infty$), then the polynomial must have even degree. If the ends head in different directions (one up and the other down), then the polynomial must have odd degree.

The graph shown in this problem is therefore for an even degree polynomial.

(4) The degree of a polynomial is at least one more than the number of "turning points" on its graph.

Since the graph in this problem has 3 turning points (at $x = -2, -1$, and approximately $\frac{1}{2}$), the degree of the polynomial must be at least 4.

162

(5) Putting notes (3) and (4) together, we see that the possible degrees for the polynomial whose graph is shown are 4, 6, 8,...

* Quick solution: Since the graph does not pass through the x-axis at the zero $x = -2$, it follows that -2 is a zero with even multiplicity. Equivalently, the factor $(x + 2)$ must appear an even number of times (or equivalently, it must have an even power). This eliminates choices A, B and D. So the answer is choice C.

Notes: (1) c is a **zero** of a polynomial $p(x)$ if $p(c) = 0$. For example, all of the polynomials in the answer choices have the same zeros. They are -2, 0 and 1.

(2) $p(c) = 0$ if and only if $x - c$ is a factor of the polynomial $p(x)$.

(3) The multiplicity of the zero x is the degree of the factor $x - c$.

For example, in choice D, 0 and 1 have multiplicity 2, and -2 has multiplicity 3.

(4) If a zero c of a polynomial has odd multiplicity, then the graph of the polynomial passes through the x-axis at $x = c$.

From the graph given, we see that 0 and 1 are zeros of the polynomial with odd multiplicity.

(5) If a zero c of a polynomial has even multiplicity, then then the graph of the polynomial touches the x-axis at $x = c$, but does not pass through it.

From the graph given, we see that -2 is a zero of the polynomial with even multiplicity.

(6) It might be tempting to try to plug in the zeros to try to eliminate answer choices in this problem. Unfortunately, all of the answer choices have polynomials with the same zeros.

147. The expression $\frac{3x-5}{x+2}$ is equivalent to which of the following?

(A) $\frac{3-5}{2}$

(B) $3 - \frac{5}{2}$

(C) $3 - \frac{5}{x+2}$

(D) $3 - \frac{11}{x+2}$

Solution using synthetic division:

$$-2 \rfloor \quad 3 \quad -5$$
$$\underline{\qquad\qquad -6}$$
$$3 \quad -11$$

So $\dfrac{3x-5}{x+2} = 3 - \dfrac{11}{x+2}$, choice D.

Notes: (1) We can use a procedure called **synthetic division** whenever we divide any polynomial by a linear polynomial of the form $x - r$.

If we are dividing by $x - r$, then we begin by writing r in the upper left hand corner. In this problem $r = -2$.

Next we make sure that the polynomial we are dividing is written in descending order of exponents (which it is) and that every exponent is accounted for (which they are). We then write down the coefficients of this polynomial. So we have the following:

$$-2 \rfloor \quad 3 \quad -5$$

We begin by bringing down the 3.

$$-2 \rfloor \quad 3 \quad -5$$
$$\underline{\qquad\qquad}$$
$$3$$

We now multiply this number by the number in the upper left. So we have $(3)(-2) = -6$. We place this number under the -5.

$$-2 \rfloor \quad 3 \quad -5$$
$$\underline{\qquad\qquad -6}$$
$$3$$

Next we add -5 and -6.

$$-2 \rfloor \quad 3 \quad -5$$
$$\underline{\qquad\qquad -6}$$
$$3 \quad -11$$

The bottom row gives the coefficients of the quotient (which is a polynomial of 1 degree less than the dividend) and the remainder.

So the quotient polynomial is the constant 3 and the remainder is -11.

We put the remainder over the linear divisor and add it to the quotient.

So we have $\frac{3x-5}{x+2} = 3 + \frac{-11}{x+2} = 3 - \frac{11}{x+2}$.

(2) This problem can also be solved using long division. This procedure is more time consuming than synthetic division, so I will omit it here and leave it as an optional exercise for the interested reader.

* Clever solution: $\frac{3x-5}{x+2} = \frac{3(x+2)-6-5}{x+2} = \frac{3(x+2)}{x+2} - \frac{11}{x+2} = 3 - \frac{11}{x+2}$.

This is choice D.

Notes: (1) We replaced x by $(x + 2)$ to match the denominator. By doing this we "accidentally" added $3 \cdot 2 = 6$ to the numerator. So we subtract 6 to "undo the damage" we caused.

(2) This problem can also be solved by picking numbers. I leave this solution as an exercise for the reader.

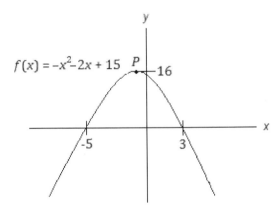

148. Which of the following is an equivalent form of the function f whose graph is shown above in the xy-plane, from which the coordinates of vertex P can be identified as constants in the equation?

$\quad$ (A) $f(x) = -(x - (-1))^2 + 16$
$\quad$ (B) $f(x) = -x(x + 2) + 15$
$\quad$ (C) $f(x) = (x + 5)(x - 3)$
$\quad$ (D) $f(x) = (x + 5)(3 - x)$

*Quick solution: The question is asking us to write the equation of the parabola in standard form. The only answer choice that is in standard form is choice A.

Note: The standard form for a quadratic function is

$$y - k = a(x - h)^2 \quad \text{or} \quad y = a(x - h)^2 + k$$

The graph is a parabola with **vertex** at (h, k). The parabola opens upwards if $a > 0$ and downwards if $a < 0$.

For example, the function f defined by $f(x) = -(x - (-1))^2 + 16$ is in standard form (this is choice A). The graph of this function is a downward facing parabola with vertex $(-1, 16)$. Here we have $h = -1$ and $k = 16$. Observe that the point $(-1, 16)$ seems to be the vertex of the parabola shown in the graph.

Algebraic solution: $y = -x^2 - 2x + 15 = -(x^2 + 2x) + 15$

$$= -(x^2 + 2x + 1) + 1 + 15 = -(x + 1)^2 + 16 = -\left(x - (-1)\right)^2 + 16$$

This is choice A.

Notes: (1) The **general form** for the equation of a parabola is

$$y = ax^2 + bx + c.$$

The equation we are given in this problem is in general form.

This form however is not that useful for identifying specific information about the parabola such as the vertex.

For this purpose, one of the following standard forms is better.

$$y = a(x - h)^2 + k, \text{ or equivalently, } y - k = a(x - h)^2$$

In either of these forms, we can identify the vertex of the parabola as (h, k).

(2) To change an equation of a parabola from general form to standard form, we use a procedure called **completing the square**. See problem 119 for a more straightforward example of completing the square.

Recall that to complete the square on the expression $x^2 + bx$, we take half of the number b, and square the result to get b^2.

For example, to complete the square on $x^2 + 2x$, we take half of 2 to get 1, and then square 1 to get $1^2 = 1$.

We then add this to the original expression to get $x^2 + 2x + 1$. This new expression is a perfect square. In fact, it factors as follows:

$$x^2 + 2x + 1 = (x + 1)(x + 1) = (x + 1)^2$$

Note that the number 1 is the same as the number we got from taking half of 2. This is not a coincidence. It always happens.

(3) We must have an expression of the form $x^2 + bx$ before completing the square. In other words, there *cannot* be a number in front of x^2 (in technical terms, the coefficient of x^2 must be 1).

In the given problem there is a coefficient of -1 in front of x^2 (note that $-x^2 = -1x^2$). We can deal with this by factoring -1 from the expression:

$$f(x) = -x^2 - 2x + 15 = -(x^2 + 2x - 15)$$

(4) Completing the square *does not* produce an expression that is equivalent to the original expression. For example, the expression $(x + 1)^2 = x^2 + 2x + 1$ is 1 more than the original expression $x^2 + 2x$.

We can fix this problem in two different ways:

<u>Method 1</u>: Add and subtract what we need inside the parentheses

Using this method, we write $f(x) = -(x^2 + 2x + 1 - 1 - 15)$.

Notice how we added and subtracted 1 inside the parentheses.

We can now simplify this expression to

$$f(x) = -(x^2 + 2x + 1 - 16)$$
$$= -(x^2 + 2x + 1) + 16$$
$$= -(x + 1)^2 + 16$$

Note how we distributed the -1 to $(x^2 + 2x + 1)$ and (-16), a slightly unconventional use of the distributive property.

<u>Method 2</u>: Add what we need inside the parentheses and adjust the other constant accordingly.

Using this method, we write $f(x) = -(x^2 + 2x + 1 - 16)$.

Since we added 1, we adjusted the -15 by subtracting 1, i.e. we have $-15 - 1 = -16$.

Now proceed as in Method 1 to put the equation in standard form.

(5) If you don't like dealing with the -1 on the right hand side of the equation, it can temporarily be moved to the left before completing the square as follows:

We rewrite $f(x) = -(x^2 + 2x - 15)$ as $-f(x) = x^2 + 2x - 15$.

Now complete the square on $x^2 + 2x$ to get $x^2 + 2x + 1$. So we need to add 1 to the right hand side of the equation. We can undo this by either (i) subtracting 1 from the same side (as in Method 1 above), (ii) adjusting the -15 to -16 (as in Method 2 above), or (iii) adding 1 to the left hand side to balance the equation.

Let's use (iii) this time and write $-f(x) = x^2 + 2x - 15$ as

$$-f(x) + 1 = x^2 + 2x + 1 - 15$$

After completing the square we have $-f(x) + 1 = (x + 1)^2 - 15$.

Subtracting 1 gives $-f(x) = (x + 1)^2 - 16$.

Finally, multiplying by -1 yields $f(x) = -(x + 1)^2 + 16$.

(6) Once the equation is in the standard form

$$f(x) = -(x + 1)^2 + 16 \quad \text{or} \quad f(x) - 16 = -(x + 1)^2$$

we can easily pick out the vertex by matching the equation up with the standard form

$$y = a(x - h)^2 + k \quad \text{or} \quad y - k = a(x - h)^2$$

Observe that $h = -1$ and $k = 16$.

(9) It is very common for students to make sign errors here. Note that the expression $(x + 1)^2$ indicates that $h = -1$, whereas the expression $f(x) - 16$ indicates that $k = 16$.

149. What is the sum of all values of k that satisfy $2k^2 - 34k + 6 = 0$?

* We divide each side of the equation by 2 to get $k^2 - 17k + 3 = 0$. The sum we are looking for is the negative of the coefficient of k in the equation, i.e. the answer is **17**.

Notes: (1) If r and s are the solutions of the quadratic equation $x^2 + bx + c = 0$, then $b = -(r + s)$ and $c = rs$. So in this problem the sum of the two solutions is 17 and the product of the two solutions is 3.

(2) Yes, you can also solve the equation $2k^2 - 34k + 6 = 0$ by completing the square or using the quadratic formula, but this is very time consuming. It is much better to use the quick solution given above.

150. If $(2x + m)(kx + n) = 6x^2 + 29x + c$ for all values of x, and $m + n = 13$, what is the value of c ?

* We need $2k = 6$. So $k = 3$. We now have

$$(2x + m)(3x + n) = 6x^2 + 29x + c$$

We need $2n + 3m = 29$.

We can now either use trial and error or formally solve the following system of equations:

$$3m + 2n = 29$$
$$m + n = 13$$

to get $m = 3$ and $n = 10$

It follows that $c = mn = 3 \cdot 10 = \mathbf{30}$.

Notes: (1) $(2x + m)(kx + n) = 2kx^2 + (2n + mk)x + mn$

(2) Using Note (1), we have

$$2kx^2 + (2n + mk)x + mn = 6x^2 + 29x + c$$

(3) using Note (2) and equating coefficients of each power of x, we have

$$2k = 6 \qquad\qquad 2n + mk = 29 \qquad\qquad mn = c$$

(4) The first equation in Note (3) gives us $k = \dfrac{6}{2} = 3$.

(5) Substituting $k = 3$ in to the second equation gives us $2n + 3m = 29$.

(6) We can solve the system of equations that appears in the solution formally using the elimination method. We can start by multiplying each side of the second equation by -2.

$$3m + 2n = 29$$
$$-2(m + n) = 13(-2)$$

We now distribute the -2 on the left, and add the two equations.

$$3m + 2n = 29$$
$$-2m - 2n = -26$$
$$m = 3$$

Since $m + n = 13$, we must have $n = 13 - m = 13 - 3 = 10$.

$$x^2 + y^2 - 6x + 2y = -6$$

151. The equation of a circle in the xy-plane is shown above. What is the radius of the circle?

* **Solution by completing the square:** We put the equation into standard form by completing the square twice:

$$x^2 - 6x + 9 + y^2 + 2y + 1 = -6 + 9 + 1$$
$$(x - 3)^2 + (y + 1)^2 = 4$$

So the radius of the circle is **2**.

Notes: (1) The given equation has a graph which is a circle, a point, or empty. On the SAT it will most likely be a circle.

(2) The **general form** for the equation of a circle is

$$x^2 + Bx + y^2 + Cy + D = 0.$$

This form is not that useful for identifying specific information about the circle such as its center and radius.

(3) The **standard form** for the equation of a circle is

$$(x - h)^2 + (y - k)^2 = r^2$$

In this form, we can identify the center as (h, k) and the radius as r.

(4) To change an equation of a circle from general form to standard form, we use a procedure called **completing the square**. See problem 119 for a more straightforward example of completing the square.

To complete the square on the expression $x^2 + bx$, we take half of the number b, and square the result to get b^2.

For example, to complete the square on $x^2 - 6x$, we take half of -6 to get -3, and then square -3 to get $(-3)^2 = 9$.

We then add this to the original expression to get $x^2 - 6x + 9$. This new expression is a perfect square. In fact, it factors as follows:

$$x^2 - 6x + 9 = (x - 3)(x - 3) = (x - 3)^2$$

Note that the number -3 is the same as the number we got from taking half of -6. This is not a coincidence. It always happens.

When we complete the square on $y^2 + 2y$, we take half of 2 to get 1, and then square 1 to get $(1)^2 = (1)(1) = 1$.

We then add this to the original expression to get $y^2 + 2y + 1$. This new expression is also a perfect square. In fact, it factors as follows:

$$y^2 + 2y + 1 = (y + 1)(y + 1) = (y + 1)^2$$

Notice again the number 1 appearing in this final expression.

(5) Completing the square *does not* produce an expression that is equivalent to the original expression. For example, the expression $(x - 3)^2 = x^2 - 6x + 9$ is 9 more than the original expression $x^2 - 6x$.

We fix this problem by adding the same quantity (in this case 9) to the other side of the equation.

(6) Once the equation is in the standard form

$$(x - 3)^2 + (y + 1)^2 = 4$$

we can easily pick out the center and radius by matching the equation up with the standard form

$$(x - h)^2 + (y - k)^2 = r^2.$$

Observe that $h = 3$, $k = -1$, and $r = 2$.

(7) It is very common for students to make sign errors here. Note that the expression $(x - 3)^2$ indicates that $h = 3$, whereas the expression $(y + 1)^2$ indicates that $k = -1$.

To see this, note that $(y + 1)^2 = (y - (-1))^2$.

(8) Another common mistake is to say that $r = 4$. This is not true!

$$r^2 = 4, \text{ so that } r = 2.$$

152. The equation $\frac{54x^2+85x-32}{kx-3} = -27x - 2 - \frac{38}{kx-3}$ is true for all values of $x \neq \frac{3}{k}$, where k is a constant. What is the value of $|k|$?

* Quick algebraic solution: We multiply each side of the equation by $kx - 3$ to get

$$54x^2 + 85x - 32 = (-27x - 2)(kx - 3) - 38$$

$$54x^2 + 85x - 32 = -27kx^2 + (81 - 2k)x + 6 - 38.$$

So we must have $-27k = 54$, and so $k = -2$. Therefore $|k| = \mathbf{2}$.

Note: We could also solve $81 - 2k = 85$ to get $k = -2$.

LEVEL 5: PROBLEM SOLVING AND DATA

153. A business is owned by 1 man and 5 women, each of whom has an equal share. If one of the women sells $\frac{2}{5}$ of her share to the man, and another of the women keeps $\frac{1}{4}$ of her share and sells the rest to the man, what fraction of the business will the man own?

    (A) $\frac{9}{40}$

    (B) $\frac{37}{120}$

    (C) $\frac{2}{3}$

    (D) $\frac{43}{120}$

Solution by changing fractional parts to wholes: Using the answer choices as a guide we will split the business into 120 parts, so that each person has $\frac{120}{6} = 20$ parts. We have $(\frac{2}{5})(20) = 8$ and $(\frac{3}{4})(20) = 15$. So after both sales the man has $20 + 8 + 15 = 43$ parts out of 120 parts total. Thus, the answer is choice D.

Remark: The number 120 comes from multiplying the least common denominator of the two fractions ($5 \cdot 4 = 20$) by the number of people (6).

* Direct solution: This is quick, but a bit tricky. Each of the 6 people begins with $\frac{1}{6}$ of the business. The first woman sells $\left(\frac{2}{5}\right)\left(\frac{1}{6}\right)$ of the business, and the second woman sells $\left(\frac{3}{4}\right)\left(\frac{1}{6}\right)$ of the business (if she keeps $\frac{1}{4}$, then she sells $\frac{3}{4}$). Therefore, we can get the answer by doing the following single computation in our calculator (if a calculator is allowed):

$$\frac{1}{6} + \left(\frac{2}{5}\right)\left(\frac{1}{6}\right) + \left(\frac{3}{4}\right)\left(\frac{1}{6}\right) = \frac{43}{120}$$

This is choice D.

154. In Dr. Steve's Calculus class, students are given a grade between 0 and 100, inclusive on each quiz. Tommy's average (arithmetic mean) for the first 8 quizzes was 86. What is the lowest grade Tommy can receive on his 9th quiz and still be able to have an average of 90 for the first 12 quizzes?

* Solution by changing averages to sums: The sum of 8 quiz grades was $86 \cdot 8 = 688$.

We want the sum of Tommy's first 12 quiz grades to be $90 \cdot 12 = 1080$.

So we need the sum of the grades on the last four quizzes to be

$$1080 - 688 = 392.$$

The maximum grade is 100, and so the most Tommy can score on the last 3 quizzes is $100 \cdot 3 = 300$.

Therefore, on the 9th quiz he must score at least $392 - 300 = \mathbf{92}$.

Note: See problem 124 for more information on changing averages to sums.

155. * The price of a government issued bond is worth \$750 today. A brokerage firm believes that the bond will lose 14% of its value each month for the next four months. The firm uses the equation $A = 750(r)^t$ to model the value, A, of the bond after t months. To the nearest dollar, what does the firm believe the bond will be worth at the end of four months?

* $r = 1 - .14 = 0.86$. It follows that $A = 750(0.86)^4 = 410.25612$. To the nearest dollar this is **410**.

Notes: (1) We can also find the value of r by picking a number as follows: After 1 month, the bond should lose 14% of its value. So if we let $t = 1$, then $A = 645$. So we have $645 = 750(r)^1 = 750r$. So $r = \frac{645}{750} = .86$.

(2) To take away 14% is the same as taking 86%. Indeed, $100 - 14 = 86$. So we can find A when $t = 1$ by multiplying 0.86 by 750 to get 645.

(3) We can also take 14% away from 750 by first computing 14% of 750, and then subtracting the result from 750.

$$.14 \cdot 750 = 105$$
$$750 - 105 = 645$$

Questions 156 - 157 refer to the following information.

$$L = \lambda W$$

For a stable system (a system is stable if the arrival rate is equal to the departure rate), Little's law is given by the above formula, where L is average number of customers in the system at any given time, λ is the average effective arrival rate, and W is the average amount of time a customer spends in the system.

The manager of Great Savings bank estimates that during business hours, an average of 2 customers per minute enter the bank and that each of them stays an average of 15 minutes. By Little's law, there are approximately 30 customers in the bank at any time.

156. Little's law can be applied to any part of the bank, such as the customer service area or the teller windows. It is determined that during business hours, approximately 75 customers per hour speak to a bank teller at a window and each of these customers spend an average of 10 minutes in line before seeing a teller. At any time during business hours, about how many customers, on average, are waiting in line for a teller at Great Savings bank?

* 75 customers per hour is the same as $\frac{75}{60} = \frac{5}{4}$ customers per minute. By Little's law, we have $L = \lambda W = \frac{5}{4} \cdot 10 = \mathbf{25/2}$ or $\mathbf{12.5}$.

Note: We can also convert 10 minutes to $\frac{10}{60} = \frac{1}{6}$ hour, and then compute $L = \lambda W = 75 \cdot \frac{1}{6} = 25/2$ or 12.5.

157. * A new branch of Great Savings bank opens nearby. For the new branch, it is estimated that, during business hours, an average of 100 customers per hour enter the bank and each of them stays an average of 20 minutes. The average number of customers in the new branch at any time is what percent greater than the average number of customers in the original branch at any time? (Note: Ignore the percent symbol when entering your answer.)

* 100 customers per hour is the same as $\frac{100}{60} = \frac{5}{3}$ customers per minute. By Little's law, we have an estimated average of $L = \lambda W = \frac{5}{3} \cdot 20 = \frac{100}{3}$ customers in the new branch at any time.

The estimated average number of customers in the original branch at any time is 30.

So the percent change is

$$\frac{\frac{100}{3} - 30}{30} \cdot 100 \approx 11.111111$$

So we grid in **11. 1**.

Note: Here we used the percent change formula:

$$Percent\ Change = \frac{Change}{Original} \times 100$$

In this problem the Original value is 30 and the Change is $\frac{100}{3} - 30$.

Do not accidently use the "new value" of $\frac{100}{3}$ for the "change." The change is the positive difference between the original and new values.

158. The average (arithmetic mean) salary of employees at an advertising firm with P employees, in thousands of dollars, is 53, and the average salary of employees at an advertising firm with Q employees in thousands of dollars is 95. When the salaries of both firms are combined, the average salary in thousands of dollars is 83. What is the value of $\frac{P}{Q}$?

* Solution by changing averages to sums: The Sum of the salaries of employees at firm P (in thousands) is $53P$.

The Sum of the salaries of employees at firm Q (in thousands) is $95Q$.

Adding these we get the Sum of the salaries of all employees (in thousands): $53P + 95Q$.

We can also get this sum directly from the problem.

$$83(P + Q) = 83P + 83Q.$$

So we have that $53P + 95Q = 83P + 83Q$.

We get P to one side of the equation by subtracting $53P$ from each side, and we get Q to the other side by subtracting $83Q$ from each side.

$$12Q = 30P$$

We can get $\frac{P}{Q}$ to one side by performing **cross division.** We do this just like cross multiplication, but we divide instead. Dividing each side of the equation by $30Q$ will do the trick (this way we get rid of Q on the left and 30 on the right).

$$\frac{P}{Q} = \frac{12}{30} = \frac{2}{5}$$

So we can grid in **2/5 or .4.**

Note: See problem 124 for more information on changing averages to sums.

Questions 159 - 160 refer to the following information.

A zoologist is monitoring the leopard population in a controlled environment which currently contains 400 leopards. The number of leopards that the botanist expects each year, x_n, can be estimated from the number of leopards the previous year, x_p, by the following equation.

$$x_n = x_p + 0.1x_p\left(1 - \frac{x_p}{M}\right)$$

The constant M in the formula is the maximum number of leopards that can survive in the environment.

159. * If $M = 800$, what will be the number of leopards two years from now? (Round your answer to the nearest whole number.)

* We substitute $M = 800$ and $x_p = 400$ into the formula to get

$$x_n = 400 + 0.1 \cdot 400 \left(1 - \frac{400}{800}\right) = 400 + 20 = 420$$

So there will be approximately 420 leopards one year from now.

We now substitute $M = 800$ and $x_p = 420$ into the formula to get

$$x_n = 420 + 0.1 \cdot 420 \left(1 - \frac{420}{800}\right) = 420 + 19.95 = 439.95$$

We round this last number to the nearest whole number to get **440**.

160. * The zoologist would like to expand the environment that the leopards are dwelling in so that their population increases more rapidly. What is the maximum number of leopards that can survive in the expanded environment if the population increases from 400 to 430 from this year to next year?

* We substitute $x_p = 400$ and $x_n = 430$ into the formula and solve for M.

$$430 = 400 + 0.1 \cdot 400 \left(1 - \frac{400}{M}\right)$$
$$30 = 0.1 \cdot 400 \left(1 - \frac{400}{M}\right)$$
$$30 = 40 \left(1 - \frac{400}{M}\right)$$
$$\frac{3}{4} = 1 - \frac{400}{M}$$
$$-\frac{1}{4} = -\frac{400}{M}$$
$$\frac{1}{4} = \frac{400}{M}$$
$$\frac{4}{1} = \frac{M}{400}$$
$$M = \mathbf{1600}$$

Notes: (1) To get from the first to the second equation, we subtracted 400 from each side.

(2) To get from the second to the third equation, we just multiplied $0.1 \cdot 400 = 40$.

(3) To get from the third to the fourth equation, we divided each side by 40. Note that $\frac{30}{40} = \frac{3}{4}$.

(4) To get from the fourth to the fifth equation, we subtracted 1 from each side. Note that $\frac{3}{4} - 1 = \frac{3}{4} - \frac{4}{4} = \frac{3-4}{4} = -\frac{1}{4}$.

(5) To get from the fifth equation to the sixth equation, we multiplied each side by -1. Equivalently, we just dropped the minus sign from each side.

(6) To get from the sixth equation to the seventh equation, we took the reciprocal of each side. In other words, we just interchanged the numerator and denominator on each side of the equation.

(7) To get from the seventh equation to the eighth (and final) equation, we cross multiplied to get $M = 4 \cdot 400 = 1600$.

SUPPLEMENTAL PROBLEMS
QUESTIONS

Full solutions to these problems are available for free download here:
www.thesatmathprep.com/320SATprmT1.html

LEVEL 1: HEART OF ALGEBRA

$$L = 17 + 2.4M$$

1. One end of a rubber band is stapled to the bottom of a table. When an object of mass M kilograms is attached to the other end of the rubber band, the rubber band stretches to a length of L centimeters as shown in the equation above. What is M when $L = 29$?

    (A) 5
    (B) 19
    (C) 29
    (D) 86.6

2. Which of the following expressions is equal to 0 for some value of a ?

    (A) $|a - 1| + 1$
    (B) $|1 - a| + 1$
    (C) $|a + 1| + 1$
    (D) $|a - 1| - 1$

3. James solved k math problems per hour for 3 hours and Paul solved t math problems per hour for 2 hours. Which of the following represents the total number of math problems solved by James and Paul?

    (A) $2k + 3t$
    (B) $3k + 2t$
    (C) $6kt$
    (D) $5kt$

$$C = \frac{5}{9}(F - 32)$$

4. The formula above shows how a temperature F, measured in degrees Fahrenheit, relates to a temperature C, measured in degrees Celsius. Which of the following gives F in terms of C ?

    (A) $F = \frac{5}{9}(C - 32)$

    (B) $F = \frac{9}{5}C + 32$

    (C) $F = \frac{9}{5}(C - 32)$

    (D) $F = \frac{9}{5}(C + 32)$

5. If $\frac{5}{7}t = \frac{2}{5}$, what is the value of t ?

6. Each student in a classroom has exactly 2 pencils on his or her desk and the teacher has 5 pencils on her desk. There are no other pencils in the room. If there are at least 17 but no more than 21 pencils in the room, what is one possible value for the number of students in the room?

7. A hose is used to fill a swimming pool with water. When the hose is turned on, the pool fills up with water at the rate of 5 gallons per minute. If the pool initially contains 350 gallons of water, how many gallons of water will be in the pool 40 minutes after the hose is turned on?

8. Let a and b be real numbers and $i = \sqrt{-1}$. When we add $-3 + 5i$ to $a + bi$, we get $4 - 3i$. What is the value of a ?

LEVEL 1: GEOMETRY AND TRIG

9. In the standard (x, y) coordinate plane, point M with coordinates $(3, 7)$ is the midpoint of $\overline{PQ}$, and P has coordinates $(1, 9)$. What are the coordinates of Q ?

    (A) $(5, 5)$
    (B) $(-5, -5)$
    (C) $(-1, 11)$
    (D) $(4, 16)$

10. Which of the following equations represents a line that is perpendicular to the line with equation $y = -2x + 5$?

(A) $y = -2x - \frac{1}{5}$

(B) $y = -\frac{1}{2}x + 3$

(C) $y = \frac{1}{2}x - 5$

(D) $y = 2x - 5$

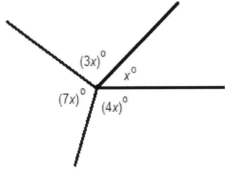

Note: Figure not drawn to scale.

11. In the figure above, four line segments meet at a point to form four angles. What is the value of x?

(A) 18
(B) 24
(C) 30
(D) 40

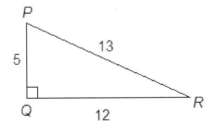

12. For $\angle P$ in $\triangle PQR$ above, which of the following trigonometric expressions has value $\frac{5}{13}$?

(A) $\sin P$
(B) $\cos P$
(C) $\tan P$
(D) $\tan R$

181

13. In isosceles triangle $\triangle PQR$, $\angle P$ and $\angle Q$ are congruent and the measure of $\angle R$ is 72°. What is the measure of $\angle P$? (Disregard the degree symbol when gridding your answer.)

14. What is the radius of a circle whose circumference is 9π ?

15. The interior dimensions of a rectangular box are 7 inches by 4 inches by 10 inches. What is the volume, in cubic inches, of the interior of the box?

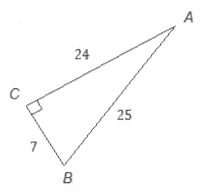

16. In the figure above, what is tan B ?

LEVEL 1: PASSPORT TO ADVANCED MATH

17. If $f(x) = 15 - 4(x + 3)$, which of the following is equivalent to $f(x)$?

   (A) $21 - 4x$
   (B) $18 - 4x$
   (C) $15 - 4x$
   (D) $3 - 4x$

18. Which of the following graphs could not be the graph of a function?

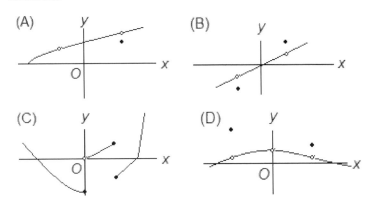

19. A cylinder has volume V, base radius r, and height h. Which of the following represents h in terms of V and r ?

    (A) $h = \dfrac{\pi V}{r^2}$

    (B) $h = \dfrac{V}{\pi r^2}$

    (C) $h = \dfrac{\pi V}{r^2}$

    (D) $h = \dfrac{\sqrt{V}}{\pi r^2}$

20. For the function $k(x) = 3x^2 - 4x + 2$, what is the value of $k(-2)$?

21. If $10xz - 15yz = az(2x - by)$ where a and b are positive real numbers, what is the value of $a + b$?

x	$p(x)$	$q(x)$	$r(x)$
1	5	6	11
2	-3	7	-10
3	-4	-7	3
4	-5	-7	-2
5	-6	0	5

22. The table above gives some values of the functions p, q, and r. At which value of x does $q(x) = p(x) + r(x)$?

23. If $xy = k$ and $y = 4$ when $x = 3$, then what is x when $y = 6$?

183

24. If $5t^2 - 35 = 13 - 3t^2$, what is the value of $7t^2$?

LEVEL 1: PROBLEM SOLVING AND DATA

Questions 25 - 27 refer to the following information.

A lion left his pride for 5 hours in search of food. The graph below shows the lion's distance from his pride over the 5-hour time period for which he was gone. The lion stopped to rest for 15 minutes and he stopped to eat for 45 minutes.

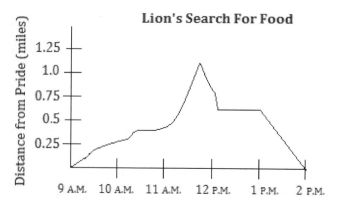

25. Based on the graph, which of the following is closest to the time the lion finished his meal?

    (A) 10:30 A.M.
    (B) 10:45 A.M.
    (C) 12:15 P.M.
    (D) 1:00 P.M.

26. During which of the following time periods was the distance between the lion and his pride strictly increasing?

    (A) Between 10:00 A.M. and 11:00 A.M.
    (B) Between 11:00 A.M. and 11:30 A.M.
    (C) Between 12:15 A.M. and 1:00 P.M.
    (D) Between 1:00 P.M. and 2:00 P.M.

27. Approximately how far was the lion from his pride while he was resting?

    (A) 0.2 miles
    (B) 0.4 miles
    (C) 0.6 miles
    (D) 0.8 miles

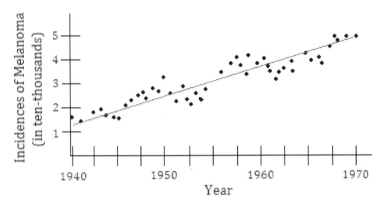

28. According to the line of best fit in the scatterplot above, which of the following best approximates the year in which the number of incidences of melanoma was estimated to be 20,000 ?

    (A) 1942
    (B) 1946
    (C) 1950
    (D) 1954

29. If y years and 7 months is equal to 439 months, what is the value of y ?

30. If a 5-pound pumpkin pie is cut into five equal pieces and each of those pieces is cut in half, what is the weight, in ounces, of each piece of pumpkin pie? (1 pound = 16 ounces)

31. A radio broadcaster sells time slots for advertising in five-minute intervals. If the radio station broadcasts advertisements for 20 minutes per hour, 24 hours per day, every day of the week, what is the total number of five-minute advertisements the broadcaster can sell for Monday through Friday?

32. A young child's height is increasing at a rate of approximately 1 inch for every three months. According to this estimate, how long will it take, in <u>years</u>, for the child's height to increase by 1 and a half feet? (1 foot = 12 inches)

LEVEL 2: HEART OF ALGEBRA

$$x + y = 1$$
$$2x + y = 3$$

33. Which of the following ordered pairs (x, y) satisfies the system of equations above?

    (A) $(-2, 3)$
    (B) $(-2, 7)$
    (C) $(2, -1)$
    (D) $(2, -2)$

34. Dana bought two blouses at a retail clothing store. The regular price for each blouse was b dollars. Dana was charged the regular price for the first blouse and she was given a 40 percent discount on the second blouse. She was charged 6 percent sales tax on the entire purchase. Which of the following expressions gives the total, in dollars, Dana paid, including sales tax?

    (A) $1.06(b - 0.4b)$
    (B) $1.06(b + 0.6b)$
    (C) $1.06(2(0.6b))$
    (D) $1.06b + 0.6b$

$$19 - \frac{3}{14}x = 7 + \frac{6}{7}x$$

35. What is the value of x in the equation above?

    (A) $\frac{14}{5}$
    (B) 7
    (C) $\frac{56}{5}$
    (D) 14

$$A = P \frac{r(1+r)^n}{(1+r)^n - 1}$$

36. The formula above gives the payment amount per period P needed to pay off an amortized loan of P dollars at r percent annual interest with a total of n payments. Which of the following gives P in terms of A, r, and n.

    (A) $P = rA$

    (B) $P = (1+r)^n A$

    (C) $P = A \frac{(1+r)^n - 1}{r(1+r)^n}$

    (D) $P = A \frac{r(1+r)^n}{(1+r)^n - 1}$

37. Which of the following numbers is NOT a solution of $\frac{1}{7}(15 + 11x) > 2x$?

    (A) 1

    (B) 3

    (C) 4

    (D) 5

38. The number of doctoral candidates in math in a large city between 1940 and 1950 was twice the number of doctoral candidates in math in the same city between 1970 and 1980. If there were 24 doctoral candidates in the city between 1940 and 1950 and there were n doctorsl candidates in the city between 1970 and 1980, which of the following equations is true?

    (A) $n + 24 = 2$

    (B) $\frac{n}{2} = 24$

    (C) $2n = 24$

    (D) $24n = 2$

39. When 6 times the number k is added to 17, the result is 35. What number results when 3 times k is added to 9 ?

$$x - 3 = \sqrt{x + k}$$

40. Given that $k = 3$, find a solution of the equation above?

LEVEL 2: GEOMETRY AND TRIG

41. Which of the following equations represents a line that is parallel to the line with equation $y = -5x - 2$?

   (A) $x + y = -2$
   (B) $x + 5y = 2$
   (C) $5x - y = -1$
   (D) $10x + 2y = 12$

42. C is the midpoint of line segment AB, and D and E are the midpoints of AC and CB, respectively. If the length of DE is 7, what is the length of AB?

   (A) 7
   (B) 10.5
   (C) 14
   (D) 17.5

43. The line $y = mx + b$, where m and b are constants, is graphed in the xy-plane. If the line contains the point (u, v) where u and v are nonzero, what is the slope of the line in terms of u and v ?

   (A) $\dfrac{b-v}{u}$

   (B) $\dfrac{v-b}{u}$

   (C) $\dfrac{b-u}{v}$

   (D) $\dfrac{u-b}{v}$

44. What is the area of a right triangle whose sides have lengths 6, 8, and 10?

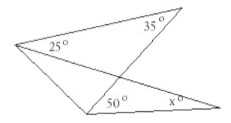

45. In the figure above, what is the value of x ?

46. The sum of 7 adjacent nonoverlapping angles is 180 degrees. Six of the angles each have a measure of y degrees and the remaining angle measures 150 degrees. What is the value of y?

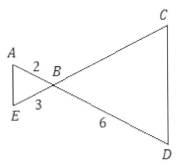

47. In the figure above, $AE \parallel CD$ and segment AD intersects segment CE at B. What is the length of segment CE ?

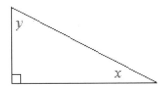

48. In the triangle above, the sine of $x°$ is 0.2. What is the cosine of $y°$?

LEVEL 2: PASSPORT TO ADVANCED MATH

$$(-7x^3 + 5x) - (-7x^3 - 5x)$$

49. Which of the following is equivalent to the expression above?

(A) 0
(B) $-14x^2$
(C) $10x$
(D) $-14x^2 + 10x$

$$h(x) = kx^4 - 7$$

50. For the function h defined above, k is a constant and $h(2) = 41$. What is the value of $h(-2)$

    (A) -41
    (B) 0
    (C) 3
    (D) 41

51. Which of the following equations has a graph in the xy-plane for which y is always greater than -3

    (A) $y = x^3 - 2$
    (B) $y = x^2 - 3$
    (C) $y = (x - 2)^2 - 3$
    (D) $y = |x - 3| - 2$

$$16x^4 + 40x^2y^2 + 25y^4$$

52. Which of the following is equivalent to the expression shown above?

    (A) $(4x + 5y)^4$
    (B) $(4x^2 + 5y^2)^2$
    (C) $(16x + 25y)^4$
    (D) $(16x^2 + 25y^2)^2$

53. What is the value of $c + 5$ if $(4c - 7) - (3 - c) = 5$?

54. If $\dfrac{12}{x-15} = \dfrac{3}{x}$, what is the value of $-3x$?

$$-x^2 + 2x - 1$$
$$2x^2 - 3x + 5$$

55. If the sum of the two polynomials given above is written in the form $ax^2 + bx + c$, then $a + b + c =$

$$3(x - 1)(2x + 5)$$

56. If we rewrite the expression above in the form $ax^2 + bx + c$, then what is the value of $b - a$?

190

LEVEL 2: PROBLEM SOLVING AND DATA

57. * The distance traveled by Mars in one orbit around the Sun is about 888,000,000 miles. Mars makes one complete orbit around the sun in approximately two Earth years. Of the following, which is the closest to the average speed of Mars, in miles per hour, as it orbits the Sun?

(A) 50,000
(B) 100,000
(C) 1,200,000
(D) 2,400,000

$$1 \text{ hectometer} = 100 \text{ meters}$$
$$10 \text{ decimeters} = 1 \text{ meter}$$

58. A farmer partitions his land into equal pieces so that each piece has a length of 5 hectometers. Based on the information given above, what is the length, in decimeters, of each piece of land?

(A) 50,000
(B) 5,000
(C) 50
(D) 0.005

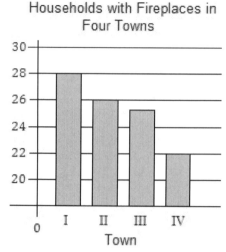

Households with Fireplaces in Four Towns

59. The number of households with fireplaces in 4 towns is shown in the graph above. If the total number of such households is 10,150, what is an appropriate label for the vertical axis of the graph?

(A) Number of households with fireplaces (in tens)
(B) Number of households with fireplaces (in hundreds)
(C) Number of households with fireplaces (in thousands)
(D) Number of households with fireplaces (in tens of thousands)

60. A survey was conducted to determine how many married couples in a large city had children. 212 couples who visited a local park on a Sunday were given the survey, and 35 couples refused to respond. Which of the following factors makes it least likely that a reliable conclusion can be drawn about the percentage of married couples in the city that have children.

(A) Population size
(B) Sample size
(C) Where the survey was given
(D) The number of people who refused to respond

61. * The *mina*, a Babylonian measure of weight, is approximately equal to 640 grams. It is also equivalent to 60 smaller Babylonian units called *talents*. Based on these relationships, 100 Babylonian talents is equivalent to how many <u>ounces</u>, to the nearest tenth? (28.35 grams = 1 ounce)

192

62. * The average (arithmetic mean) of seventeen numbers is 152. If an eighteenth number, 44, is added to the group, what is the average of the eighteen numbers?

Questions 63 - 64 refer to the following information.

A survey was conducted among a randomly chosen sample of 100 males and 100 females to gather data on pet ownership. The data are shown in the table below.

	Has pets	Does not have pets	Total
Men	75	25	100
Women	63	37	100
Total	138	62	200

63. According to the table, what is the probability that a randomly selected man does not have pets?

64. * According to the table, what is the probability that a randomly selected person with pets is female?

LEVEL 3: HEART OF ALGEBRA

65. Perfect Floors Carpeting estimates the price of a carpeting job, in dollars, using the expression $8kt + 95$, where k is the number of workers and t is the total time, in hours, needed to complete the job using k workers. Which of the following is the best interpretation of the number 8 in the expression?

(A) Each worker works for 8 hours.
(B) The price of the job increases by $8 every hour.
(C) At least 8 workers are needed to complete the job.
(D) Perfect Floors Carpeting charges $8 per hour for each worker.

193

$$2x - 5y = -28$$
$$y - x = -13$$

66. What is the solution (x, y) to the system of equations above?

(A) $(5, -8)$
(B) $(31, 18)$
(C) $(-4, 4)$
(D) $(0, -13)$

67. Which of the following numbers is NOT a solution of the inequality $5x - 7 \geq 6x - 4$

(A) -6
(B) -4
(C) -3
(D) -2

$$P = \frac{G}{G + N}$$

68. The formula above is used to compute the percentage P of people in any population that play the guitar, where G is the number of people from the population that play the guitar, and N is the number of people from the population that do not play the guitar. Which of the following expresses the number of people that play the guitar in terms of the other variables?

(A) $G = \frac{N}{P-1}$
(B) $G = \frac{N}{1-P}$
(C) $G = \frac{PN}{1-P}$
(D) $G = \frac{PN}{P-1}$

$$y > x + k$$
$$y < m - x$$

69. In the xy-plane, $(0,0)$ is a solution to the system of inequalities above. Which of the following relationships between k and m must be true?

(A) $k = -m$
(B) $k > m$
(C) $k < m$
(D) $|k| < |m|$

194

70. The exact weight of an item is x pounds, where $x > 250$ and the estimated weight of the item is y pounds. For a certain experiment to be successful, the estimated weight must be within 3 pounds of the exact weight. If the experiment is successful, which of the following inequalities represents the relationship between the exact weight and the estimated weight of the item?

    (A) $y > x + 3$
    (B) $y < x - 3$
    (C) $x + y < 3$
    (D) $-3 < y - x < 3$

71. A retailer ships two types of laptop computers. Each computer of type A weighs 5 pounds each, and each computer of type B weighs 8 pounds each. A shipment of 76 computers weighing a total of 467 pounds is sent out to a university. How many type B computers are in the shipment?

72. The daily cost C, in dollars, for a factory to produce x items can be modeled by the equation $C = \frac{x+170}{5}$. According to the model, for each new item produced, by how many <u>cents</u> does the daily cost increase?

LEVEL 3: GEOMETRY AND TRIG

73. The line m in the xy-plane contains points from each of Quadrants I, III, and IV, but no points from Quadrant II. Which of the following must be true?

    (A) The slope of line m is positive.
    (B) The slope of line m is negative.
    (C) The slope of line m is zero.
    (D) The slope of line m is undefined.

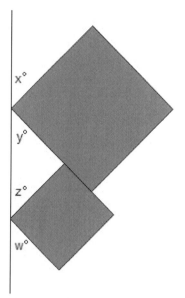

Note: Figure not drawn to scale.

74. In the figure above, the two shaded regions are squares. Which of the following must be true?

   (A) $x = y$
   (B) $x = w$
   (C) $y = z$
   (D) $y = w$

196

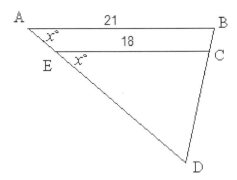

75. In the figure above, what is the value of $\frac{ED}{AD}$?

(A) $\frac{1}{7}$

(B) $\frac{1}{4}$

(C) $\frac{1}{2}$

(D) $\frac{6}{7}$

76. The volume of a right circular cylinder is 375π cubic centimeters. If the height is three times the base radius of the cylinder, what is the base <u>diameter</u> of the cylinder?

77. * Mike has identical containers each in the shape of a cone with internal diameter of 5 inches. He pours liquid from a half-gallon bottle into each container until it is full. If the height of liquid in each container is 8 inches, what is the largest number of full containers that he can pour a half-gallon of liquid? (Note: There are 231 cubic inches in 1 gallon.)

78. A rectangle has a perimeter of 22 meters and an area of 28 square meters. What is the shortest of the side lengths, in meters, of the rectangle?

79. The height of a solid cone is 22 centimeters and the radius of the base is 15 centimeters. A cut parallel to the circular base is made completely through the cone so that one of the two resulting solids is a smaller cone. If the radius of the base of the small cone is 5 centimeters, what is the height of the small cone, in centimeters?

197

80. In a right triangle, one angle measures $\theta°$, where $\sin\theta = \frac{2}{7}$. What is $\cos((90-\theta)°)$

LEVEL 3: PASSPORT TO ADVANCED MATH

$$y = x^2 - 12x + 35$$

81. The equation above represents a parabola in the xy-plane. Which of the following equivalent forms of the equation displays the x-intercepts of the parabola as constants or coefficients?

    (A) $y - 35 = x^2 - 12x$
    (B) $y - 1 = (x - 6)^2$
    (C) $y = x(x - 12) + 35$
    (D) $y = (x - 5)(x - 7)$

82. If $g(x) = -3x - 7$, what is $g(-4x)$ equal to?

    (A) $12x^2 + 28x$
    (B) $12x + 7$
    (C) $12x - 7$
    (D) $-12x + 7$

83. In the xy-plane, the graph of function g has x-intercepts at -5, -2, 2, and 5. Which of the following could define g ?

    (A) $g(x) = (x - 5)^2(x - 2)^2$
    (B) $g(x) = (x + 5)^2(x + 2)^2$
    (C) $g(x) = (x - 5)^2(x + 2)(x - 2)^3(x + 5)$
    (D) $g(x) = (x - 5)(x + 5)(x - 2)^2$

$$f(x) = kx^3 - 7$$

84. For the function f defined above, k is a constant and $f(2) = 25$. What is the value of $f(-1)$

    (A) -18
    (B) -11
    (C) 0
    (D) 18

k	-1	1	2
$f(k)$	-5	3	7

85. The table above shows some values of the linear function f. Which of the following defines f?

   (A) $f(k) = k - 4$

   (B) $f(k) = k - 8$

   (C) $f(k) = 2k - 4$

   (D) $f(k) = 4k - 1$

86. Which of the following is equivalent to the expression $(x - 7)(x - 2) + 4$?

   (A) $(x - 3)(x - 6)$
   (B) $(x - 3)(x + 6)$
   (C) $(x - 3)^2 + 4$
   (D) $x^2 - 7x - 2x + 13$

87. In the xy-plane, the graph of the function f, with equation $f(x) = cx^2 - 7$, passes through the point $(-3,38)$. What is the value of c?

$$x^2 - 2x = 15$$

88. In the quadratic equation above, find the positive solution for x.

LEVEL 3: PROBLEM SOLVING AND DATA

89. Which of the following graphs best shows a strong positive association between x and y?

(A)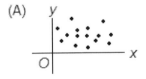

(B)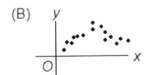

(C)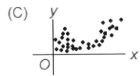

(D)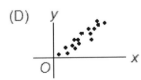

199

Questions 90 - 91 refer to the following information.

The table below lists the results of a survey of a random sample of 500 high school freshman, sophomores and juniors. Each student selected one animal that was his or her favorite.

Favorite Animals

	Dog	Cat	Elephant	Monkey	Lion	Total
Fresh	82	17	20	36	18	173
Soph	51	46	5	50	6	158
Jun	24	30	63	22	30	169
Total	157	93	88	108	54	500

90. If the sample is representative of a high school with 2,500 freshmen, sophomores and juniors, then based on the table, what is the predicted number of juniors at the high school who would select the elephant as their favorite animal?

    (A) 63
    (B) 88
    (C) 315
    (D) 845

91. * If one of the freshman from the sample is selected at random, which of the following is closest to the probability the student selected the monkey as his or her favorite animal?

    (A) 0.07
    (B) 0.21
    (C) 0.33
    (D) 0.50

200

Questions 92 - 93 refer to the following information.

The graph below displays the total cost C, in dollars, of renting a car for d days.

Total Cost of Renting a Car by the Day

92. What does the C-intercept represent in the graph?

    (A) The total number of days the cars is rented
    (B) The total number of cars rented
    (C) The initial cost of renting the car
    (D) The increase in cost to rent the car for each additional day

93. Which of the following represents the relationship between C and d ?

    (A) $d = 50C$
    (B) $C = 50d$
    (C) $C = 100d + 50$
    (D) $C = 50d + 50$

94. A tracker was implanted inside a bald eagle's wing, and its flight speed was monitored over a period of 2 hours. The data are graphed on the set of axes below with the time elapsed on the *x*-axis and the flight speed of the eagle on the *y*-axis.

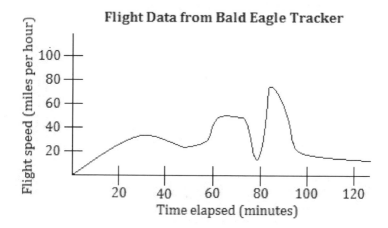

Flight Data from Bald Eagle Tracker

Based on the graph, which statement is true?

(A) The eagle's maximum flight speed is reached about 70 minutes after the observation begins.

(B) The eagle's flight speed steadily decreases between 40 and 60 minutes during the observation.

(C) The eagle's minimum flight speed during the second hour of observation is approximately 12 miles per hour.

(D) The eagle's maximum flight speed during the first hour of observation is greater than the eagle's maximum flight speed during the second hour of observation.

Mean Annual Salary of NBA Players Each Year from 1980 to 1984

95. According to the line graph above, the mean annual salary of an NBA player in 1981 was what fraction of the mean annual salary of an NBA player in 1984 ?

96. * A zoologist is studying the elephant population in two regions in Africa. He observed that Region I had 30 percent more elephants than Region II. Based on this observation, if Region I had 741 elephants, then how many elephants were in region II?

LEVEL 4: HEART OF ALGEBRA

$$3x - ky = 7$$
$$kx + 12y = 5$$

97. In the system of equations above, k is a constant and x and y are variables. For what real value of k will the system of equations have no real solution?

(A) -6

(B) 0

(C) 6

(D) There is no such value of k.

203

98. If $a^{\frac{3}{7}} = b$, what does a^9 equal in terms of b?

    (A) b^3

    (B) $b^{\frac{27}{7}}$

    (C) b^7

    (D) b^{21}

99. Packages of two different weights are loaded into a freight elevator. Each of the lighter packages weighs 27 pounds, and each of the heavier packages weighs 53 pounds. Let x be the number of lighter packages on the elevator and let y be the number of heavier packages on the elevator. The freight elevator can support a maximum weight of 1,800 pounds and it has enough space for a total of 36 packages. Which of the following systems of inequalities represents this relationship?

    (A) $\begin{cases} x + y \leq 1{,}800 \\ 27x + 53y \leq 36 \end{cases}$

    (B) $\begin{cases} x + y \leq 36 \\ 27x + 53y \leq 1{,}800 \end{cases}$

    (C) $\begin{cases} \frac{x}{27} + \frac{y}{53} \leq 1{,}800 \\ x + y \leq 36 \end{cases}$

    (D) $\begin{cases} x + y \leq 1{,}800 \\ 27x + 53y \leq 1{,}800 \end{cases}$

100. If $a \neq 13$ and $\frac{a^2 - 169}{a - 13} = b^2$, what does a equal in terms of b ?

    (A) $b^2 - 13$

    (B) $b^2 + 13$

    (C) $\sqrt{b} - \sqrt{13}$

    (D) $b - \sqrt{13}$

101. A carpenter spent a total of $5.44 for nails and screws. Each screw cost 2 times as much as each nail, and the carpenter bought 6 times as many nails as screws. How much, in dollars, did the customer spend on screws? (Disregard the $ sign when gridding your answer.)

204

102. If $i = \sqrt{-1}$, and $\frac{(3+i)}{(1-7i)} = a + bi$, where a and b are real numbers, then what is the value of $25(a + b)$?

103. If $15 < |b - 11| < 16$ and $b < 0$, what is one possible value of $|b|$?

104. * If $x = 2\sqrt{3}$ and $5x = \sqrt{27y}$, what is the value of y ?

LEVEL 4: GEOMETRY AND TRIG

105. A container in the shape of a right circular cylinder has an inside base radius of 5 centimeters and an inside height of 6 centimeters. This cylinder is completely filled with fluid. All of the fluid is then poured into a second right circular cylinder with a larger inside base radius of 7 centimeters. What must be the minimum inside height, in centimeters, of the second container?

(A) $\frac{5}{\sqrt{7}}$

(B) $\frac{7}{5}$

(C) 5

(D) $\frac{150}{49}$

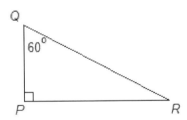

106. In the triangle above, $QR = 8$. What is the area of $\triangle PQR$?

(A) $32\sqrt{3}$
(B) 32
(C) $16\sqrt{3}$
(D) $8\sqrt{3}$

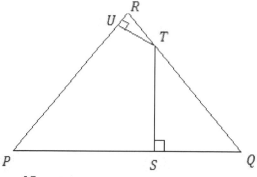

Note: Figure not drawn to scale.

107. Triangle *PQR* above is equilateral with *PQ* = 55. The ratio of *ST* to *TU* is 7 : 4. What is the length of $\overline{SQ}$?

    (A) 8

    (B) $\frac{35}{2}$

    (C) $\frac{35\sqrt{3}}{2}$

    (D) 35

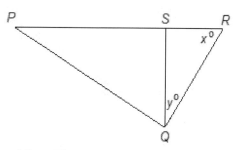

Note: Figure not drawn to scale.

108. In the figure above, if *x* = 35, *PQ* ⊥ *QR*, and *PQ* = *PS*, what is the value of *y* ?

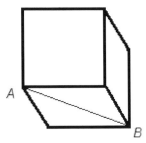

109. In the figure above, segment $\overline{AB}$ joins two vertices of the cube. If the length of $\overline{AB}$ is $3\sqrt{2}$, what is the surface area of the cube?

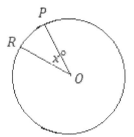

Note: Figure not drawn to scale.

110. * In the figure above, O is the center of the circle, and the radius of the circle is 8. If the length of arc $\overset{\frown}{PR}$ is between 3 and 4, what is one possible <u>integer</u> value of x ?

111. What is the area of a square whose diagonal has length $5\sqrt{2}$?

112. Suppose that $0 < k < 90$, $0 < t < 90$, and $\cos k° = \sin t°$. If $k = \frac{1}{3}z - 42$ and $t = \frac{2}{3}z + 12$, what is the value of z ?

LEVEL 4: PASSPORT TO ADVANCED MATH

$$y = ax^2 - b$$
$$y = 5$$

113. In the system of equations above, a and b are constants. For which of the following values of a and b does the system of equations have no real solutions?
    (A) $a = -2, b = -6$
    (B) $a = 2, b = -6$
    (C) $a = 2, b = -4$
    (D) $a = 2, b = 4$

114. If $k \neq \pm 1$, which of the following is equivalent to $\dfrac{1}{\frac{1}{k+1}+\frac{1}{k-1}}$.

(A) $2k$

(B) $k^2 - 1$

(C) $\dfrac{k^2-1}{2k}$

(D) $\dfrac{2k}{k^2-1}$

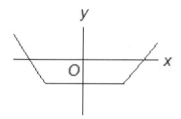

115. The graph of $y = h(x)$ is shown above. Which of the following could be the graph of $y = |h(x)|$?

(A)

(B)

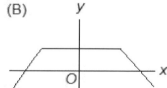

(C)

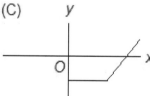

(D)

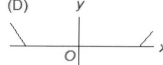

(E)

208

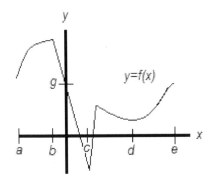

116. The figure above shows the graph of the function f on the interval $a < x < e$. Which of the following expressions represents the difference between the maximum and minimum values of $f(x)$ on this interval?

    (A) $f(b - e)$
    (B) $f(b - c)$
    (C) $f(a) - f(e)$
    (D) $f(b) - f(c)$

117. Let a, b, and c be numbers such that $-a < b < c < a$. Which of the following must be true?

    I. $c - b > 0$
  II. $b + c > 0$
 III. $|b| < a$

    (A) I only
    (B) III only
    (C) I and III only
    (D) I, II, and III

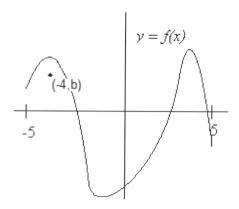

118. The figure above shows the graph of the function f and the point $(-4, b)$. For how many values of x between -5 and 5 does $f(x) = b$?

$$3x^2 + 19x = 14$$

119. If a and b are distinct solutions of the equation above, what is the value of $-3ab$?

$$y = (x + 7)(3x - 5)$$
$$x = 3y + 1$$

120. How many ordered pairs (x, y) satisfy the system of equations shown above?

LEVEL 4: PROBLEM SOLVING AND DATA

121. Juan bought a pair of sneakers at a shoe store that gave a 30 percent discount off its original price. The total amount he paid to the cashier was d dollars, including a 6 percent sales tax on the discounted price. Which of the following represents the original price of the pair of sneakers in terms of d ?

(A) $0.76d$

(B) $\dfrac{d}{0.76}$

(C) $(0.7)(1.06)d$

(D) $\dfrac{d}{(0.7)(1.06)}$

210

122. A rectangle was changed by increasing its length by r percent and decreasing its width by 20%. If these changes increased the area of the rectangle by 4%, what is the value of r ?

    (A) 10
    (B) 20
    (C) 30
    (D) 40

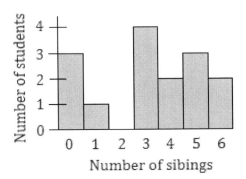

Number of sibings

123. * The histogram above shows the distribution of the number of siblings that each of 15 students has. Which of the following is true for this group of 15 students?

    I. The range of the number of siblings is greater than the mean number of siblings.
    II. The mean number of siblings is greater than the mode number of siblings.
    III. The mode number of siblings is greater than the median number of siblings.

    (A) I and II only
    (B) I and III only
    (C) II and III only
    (D) I, II, and III

211

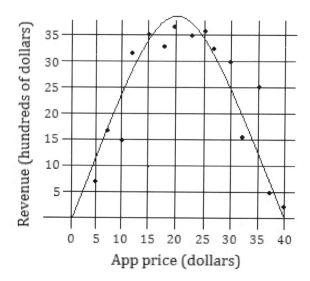

App price (dollars)

124. A tech company released a new app and wanted to determine a price that would maximize their revenue. They tested a different price each week for 15 weeks. The scatterplot above shows the app's prices and the revenue taken in by the company when the app was made available at those different prices. A quadratic model that best fits the data is also shown. For a price of $35, which of the following best approximates the percent decrease from the test revenue to the revenue that the model predicts?

(A) 200%
(B) 100%
(C) 75%
(D) 50%

125. Which scatterplot shows a relationship that is appropriately modeled with the equation $y = ab^x$, where $a > 0$ and $b > 1$?

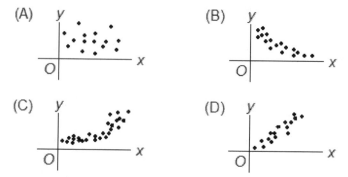

212

Questions 126 – 127 refer to the following information.

At the beginning of July, 58 percent of the animals in a shelter were dogs, and the rest were cats. By the end of July, 45 percent of the dogs and 63 percent of the cats were adopted.

126. * What percentage of the animals in the shelter were adopted? (Ignore the percent symbol when entering your answer. For example, if the answer is 12.3%, enter 12.3)

127. * What percentage of the animals that were adopted were cats? (Ignore the percent symbol when entering your answer. For example, if the answer is 12.3%, enter 12.3)

	At least 6 feet tall	Less than 6 feet tall
Male		
Female		
Total	15	34

128. * The incomplete table above classifies the number of students by height for the twelfth-grade students at Washington High School. There are twice as many male students that are less than 6 feet tall as there are male students that are at least 6 feet tall, and there are four times as many female students that are less than 6 feet tall as there are female students that are at least 6 feet tall. What is the probability that a randomly selected student that is at least 6 feet tall is female?

LEVEL 5: HEART OF ALGEBRA

129. If $x^2 - y^2 = 10 - k - 3k^2$, $x - y = 5 - 3k$, and $k \neq \frac{5}{3}$, what is $x + y$ in terms of k?

(A) $k - 2$
(B) $(k - 2)^2$
(C) $k + 2$
(D) $(k + 2)^2$

130. If $x^2 = 9$ and $y^2 = 5$, then $(2x + y)^2$ could equal which of the following?

    (A) 41
    (B) 61
    (C) $61 - 12\sqrt{5}$
    (D) $41 + 12\sqrt{5}$

$$k = a - b + 13$$
$$k = b - c - 11$$
$$k = c - d + 15$$
$$k = d - a + 11$$

131. In the system of equations above, what is the value of k ?

132. If $2x = 7 - 3y$ and $5y = 5 - 3x$, what is the value of x?

Questions 133 - 134 refer to the following information.

The quantity of a product supplied (called the *supply*) and the quantity of the product demanded (called the *demand*) in an economic market are functions of the price of the product. The market is said to be in *equilibrium* when the supply and demand are equal. The price at equilibrium is called the *equilibrium price*, and the quantity at equilibrium is called the *equilibrium demand*. Consider the following supply and demand functions where p is the price, in dollars, s is the supply function, and d is the demand function.

$$s = \frac{2}{3}p + 15$$
$$d = -\frac{1}{3}p + 99$$

133. What is the equilibrium price? (Disregard the dollar sign when gridding your answer.)

134. What is the equilibrium demand?

$$y \geq -12x + 600$$
$$y \geq 3x$$

135. In the xy-plane, if a point with coordinates (a, b) lies in the solution set of the system of inequalities above, what is the minimum possible value of b?

136. Each day, a factory's total expenses are equal to a fixed daily expense plus a variable expense that is directly proportional to the number of units of product produced by the factory during that day. If the factory's total expenses for a day in which it produces 3,000 units are $5,500, and the total expenses for a day in which it produces 7,000 units are $8,200, what is the factory's fixed daily expense? (Disregard the dollar sign when gridding your answer.)

LEVEL 5: GEOMETRY AND TRIG

137. * A cube with volume 64 cubic inches is inscribed in a sphere so that each vertex of the cube touches the sphere. Which of the following is the best approximation for the length of the radius, in inches, of the sphere?

    (A) 1.5
    (B) 3
    (C) 3.5
    (D) 7

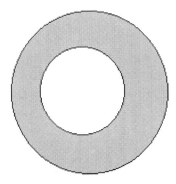

138. A circular disk is cut out of a larger circular disk, as shown in the figure above, so that the area of the piece that remains is the same as the area of the cutout. If the radius of the larger circle is R, what is the circumference of the cutout, in terms of R ?

    (A) $R\pi$
    (B) $R\sqrt{2}$
    (C) $R\pi\sqrt{2}$
    (D) $2R\pi\sqrt{2}$

215

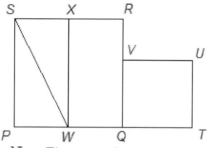

Note: Figure not drawn to scale.

139. In the figure above, $PQRS$ and $QTUV$ are squares, W and X are the midpoints of $\overline{PQ}$ and $\overline{RS}$, respectively, and $TW = SW$. If $RX = \frac{1}{2}$, what is the length of $\overline{UV}$?

    (A) $\frac{\sqrt{5}-1}{2}$

    (B) $\frac{\sqrt{3}-1}{2}$

    (C) $\frac{\sqrt{5}}{2}$

    (D) $\frac{\sqrt{3}}{2}$

140. The vertex of $\angle P$ is the origin of the standard (x, y) coordinate plane. One ray of $\angle P$ is the positive x-axis. The other ray, $\overrightarrow{PQ}$, is positioned so that $\tan A < 0$ and $\sin A > 0$. In which quadrant, if it can be determined, is point Q ?

    (A) Quadrant I
    (B) Quadrant II
    (C) Quadrant III
    (D) Cannot be determined from the given information

141. If the diameter of a circle is doubled, by what percent is the area of the circle increased? (Disregard the percent symbol when you grid your answer.)

142. The circumference of the base of a right circular cone is 10π and the circumference of a parallel cross section is 8π. If the distance between the base and the cross section is 6, what is the height of the cone?

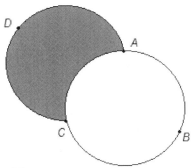

Note: Figure not drawn to scale.

143. In the above figure, arcs ABC and ADC each measure 270 degrees and each of these arcs is part of a circle of radius 8 inches. What is the area of the shaded region to the nearest inch?

144. For any cube, if the volume is V cubic centimeters and the surface area is S square centimeters, then S is directly proportional to V^n for $n =$

LEVEL 5: PASSPORT TO ADVANCED MATH

$$x^2 + \frac{2c}{3}x = 3t$$

145. In the quadratic equation above, c and t are constants. What are the solutions for x ?

(A) $x = \dfrac{-c \pm \sqrt{c^2 + 9t}}{3}$

(B) $x = \dfrac{-c \pm \sqrt{c^2 + 27t}}{3}$

(C) $x = \dfrac{-c \pm \sqrt{3c^2 + 27t}}{3}$

(D) $x = -c \pm \sqrt{c^2 + 3t}$

217

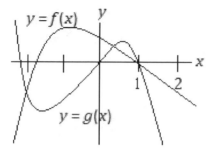

146. Graphs of the functions f and g are shown in the xy-plane above. For which of the following values of x does $f(x) + g(x) = 0$?

(A) -2
(B) -1
(C) 0
(D) $\frac{1}{2}$

$$g(x) = x^2 + 2x + 1$$
$$h(x) = 2x^3 + 3x^2 + 2x$$

147. The polynomials g and h are defined above. Which of the following polynomials is divisible by $2x + 1$?

(A) $k(x) = g(x) + h(x)$
(B) $k(x) = g(x) + 3h(x)$
(C) $k(x) = 2g(x) + h(x)$
(D) $k(x) = 2g(x) + 3h(x)$

148. What are the solutions to $5x^2 - 30x + 20 = 0$?

(A) $x = -20 \pm 20\sqrt{5}$
(B) $x = -20 \pm \sqrt{5}$
(C) $x = 3 \pm 20\sqrt{5}$
(D) $x = 3 \pm \sqrt{5}$

149. For all positive integers x, the function f is defined by $f(x) = (\frac{1}{b^5})^x$, where b is a constant greater than 1. Which of the following is equivalent to $f(3x)$?

(A) $\sqrt[3]{f(x)}$
(B) $(f(x))^3$
(C) $3f(x)$
(D) $\frac{1}{3}f(x)$

218

$$x^5 - 4x^3 + 3x^2 - 12 = 0$$

150. For what positive real value of x is the equation above true?

$$y = p(x + 3)(x - 5)$$

151. In the quadratic equation above, p is a nonzero constant. The graph of the equation in the xy-plane is a parabola with vertex (h, k). What is the value of $h - \dfrac{k}{p}$?

152. If the expression $\dfrac{x^3 - 5x^2 + 3x + 9}{x - 1}$ is written in the equivalent form $ax^2 + bx + c + \dfrac{d}{x-1}$, what is the value of d?

LEVEL 5: PROBLEM SOLVING AND DATA

$$2x, 6.1, 5.7, x, 2.3$$

153. The five numbers shown are listed in decreasing order. Which of the following values could be the range of the six numbers?

(A) 2.7
(B) 3.5
(C) 8.3
(D) 9.2

154. There are m bricks that need to be stacked. After n of them have been stacked, then in terms of m and n, what percent of the bricks have not yet been stacked?

(A) $\dfrac{m}{100(m-n)}$ %
(B) $\dfrac{100(m-n)}{m}$ %
(C) $\dfrac{100m}{n}$ %
(D) $\dfrac{100n}{m}$ %

155. * If Ted's weight increased by 36 percent and Jessica's weight decreased by 22 percent during a certain year, the ratio of Ted's weight to Jessica's weight at the end of the year was how many times the ratio at the beginning of the year?

Questions 156 - 157 refer to the following information.

A biologist places a colony consisting of 5000 bacteria into a petri dish. After the initial placement of the bacteria at time $t = 0$, the biologist measures and estimates the number of bacteria present every half hour. This data was then fitted by an exponential curve of the form $y = c \cdot 2^{kt}$ where c and k are constants, t is measured in hours, and y is measured in thousands of bacteria. The scatterplot together with the exponential curve are shown below.

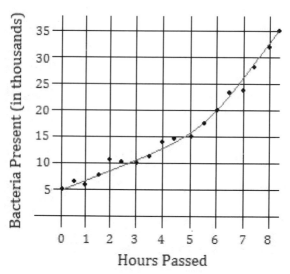

156. According to the scatterplot, the biologist's measurements indicate that the number of bacteria present quadrupled in 6 hours, and the exponential curve passes through the corresponding data point at time $t = 6$. The exponential function also agrees with the initial number of bacteria. Compute ck.

157. Suppose that the data was fitted with a quadratic function of the form $t^2 + bt + c$ instead of an exponential function. Assume that the quadratic function agrees with the scatterplot at times $t = 0$ and $t = 6$. What is the t-coordinate of the vertex of the graph of the quadratic function?

158. * The price of a government issued bond is worth $600 today. A brokerage firm believes that the bond will increase in value by 12% each month for the next six months. The firm uses the equation $A = 600(r)^t$ to model the value, A, of the bond after t months. To the nearest dollar, what does the firm believe the bond will be worth at the end of six months?

159. For 5 numbers in a list of increasing numbers, the average (arithmetic mean), median, and mode are all equal to 11. The range of the list is 7. The second number in the list is less than 11 and 2 more than the least number in the list. What is the greatest number in the list?

160. At Brilliance University, the chess team has 16 members and the math team has 13 members. If a total of 7 students belong to only one of the two teams, how many students belong to both teams?

ANSWERS TO
SUPPLEMENTAL PROBLEMS

LEVEL 1: HEART OF ALGEBRA

1. A
2. D
3. B
4. B
5. .56
6. 6, 7 or 8
7. 550
8. 7

LEVEL 1: GEOMETRY AND TRIG

9. A
10. C
11. B
12. B
13. 54
14. 9/2 or 4.5
15. 280
16. 24/7, 3.42 or 3.43

LEVEL 1: PASSPORT TO ADVANCED MATH

17. D
18. C
19. B
20. 22
21. 8
22. 4
23. 2
24. 42

LEVEL 1: PROBLEM SOLVING AND DATA

25. D
26. B

27. B
28. B
29. 36
30. 8
31. 480
32. 9/2 or 4.5

LEVEL 2: HEART OF ALGEBRA

33. C
34. B
35. C
36. C
37. D
38. C
39. 18
40. 6

LEVEL 2: GEOMETRY AND TRIG

41. D
42. C
43. B
44. 24
45. 10
46. 5
47. 12
48. 1/5 or .2

LEVEL 2: PASSPORT TO ADVANCED MATH

49. C
50. D
51. D
52. B
53. 8
54. 15
55. 4
56. 3

LEVEL 2: PROBLEM SOLVING AND DATA

57. A

58. B
59. B
60. C
61. 37.6
62. 146
63. 1/4 or .25
64. .456 or .457

LEVEL 3: HEART OF ALGEBRA

65. D
66. B
67. D
68. C
69. C
70. D
71. 29
72. 20

LEVEL 3: GEOMETRY AND TRIG

73. A
74. D
75. D
76. 10
77. 2
78. 4
79. 22/3 or 7.33
80. 2/7, .285 or .286

LEVEL 3: PASSPORT TO ADVANCED MATH

81. D
82. C
83. C
84. B
85. D
86. A
87. 5
88. 5

LEVEL 3: PROBLEM SOLVING AND DATA

89. D
90. C
91. B
92. C
93. D
94. C
95. 4/7 or .571
96. 570

LEVEL 4: HEART OF ALGEBRA

97. D
98. D
99. B
100. A
101. 1.36
102. 9
103. $4 < |b| < 5$
104. 11.1

LEVEL 4: GEOMETRY AND TRIG

105. D
106. D
107. B
108. 55/2 or 27.5
109. 54
110. 22, 23, 24, 25, 26, 27, or 28
111. 25
112. 120

LEVEL 4: PASSPORT TO ADVANCED MATH

113. B
114. C
115. A
116. D
117. C
118. 4
119. 14

120. 2

LEVEL 4: PROBLEM SOLVING AND DATA

121. D
122. C
123. A
124. D
125. C
126. 52.5 or 52.6
127. 50.3
128. 2/15 or .133

LEVEL 5: HEART OF ALGEBRA

129. C
130. D
131. 7
132. 20
133. 84
134. 71
135. 120
136. 3475

LEVEL 5: GEOMETRY AND TRIG

137. C
138. C
139. A
140. B
141. 300
142. 30
143. 165
144. 2/3, .666, or .667

LEVEL 5: PASSPORT TO ADVANCED MATH

145. B
146. B
147. C
148. D
149. B
150. 2

151. 17
152. 8

LEVEL 5: PROBLEM SOLVING AND DATA

153. C
154. B
155. 1.74
156. 5/3, 1.66 or 1.67
157. 7/4 or 1.75
158. 1184
159. 15
160. 11

ACTIONS TO COMPLETE AFTER YOU HAVE READ THIS BOOK

1. Take another practice SAT

You should see a substantial improvement in your score.

2. Continue to practice SAT math problems for 10 to 20 minutes each day

Keep practicing problems of the appropriate levels until two days before the SAT.

3. Review this book

If this book helped you, please post your positive feedback on the site you purchased it from; e.g. Amazon, Barnes and Noble, etc.

4. Claim your FREE bonuses

If you have not done so yet, visit the following webpage and enter your email address to receive additional problems with solutions.

www.thesatmathprep.com/320SATprmT1.html

About the Author

Dr. Steve Warner, a New York native, earned his Ph.D. at Rutgers University in Pure Mathematics in May, 2001. While a graduate student, Dr. Warner won the TA Teaching Excellence Award.

After Rutgers, Dr. Warner joined the Penn State Mathematics Department as an Assistant Professor. In September, 2002, Dr. Warner returned to New York to accept an Assistant Professor position at Hofstra University. By September 2007, Dr. Warner had received tenure and was promoted to Associate Professor. He has taught undergraduate and graduate courses in Precalculus, Calculus, Linear Algebra, Differential Equations, Mathematical Logic, Set Theory and Abstract Algebra.

Over that time, Dr. Warner participated in a five year NSF grant, "The MSTP Project," to study and improve mathematics and science curriculum in poorly performing junior high schools. He also published several articles in scholarly journals, specifically on Mathematical Logic.

Dr. Warner has more than 15 years of experience in general math tutoring and tutoring for standardized tests such as the SAT, ACT and AP Calculus exams. He has tutored students both individually and in group settings.

In February, 2010 Dr. Warner released his first SAT prep book "The 32 Most Effective SAT Math Strategies," and in 2012 founded Get 800 Test Prep. Since then Dr. Warner has written books for the SAT, ACT, GRE, SAT Math Subject Tests and AP Calculus exams.

Dr. Steve Warner can be reached at

steve@SATPrepGet800.com

BOOKS BY DR. STEVE WARNER

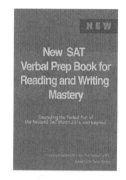

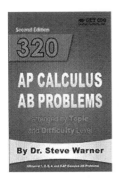
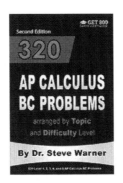
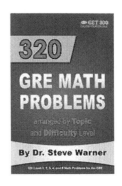

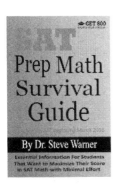

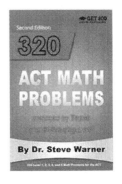

Made in the USA
San Bernardino, CA
12 August 2017